Retirement: Life's Greatest Adventure

A Retiree's Guide to a Happy, Fulfilling Life

By Bill Leavitt

Published by Write On Technical Writing, Inc., Valparaiso, Indiana

Retirement: Life's Greatest Adventure
A Retiree's Guide to a Happy, Fulfilling Life

Published by Write On Technical Writing, Inc.
417 Killarney Lane
Valparaiso, Indiana 46385
WriteOn55@aol.com

Art Credits: Cartoon illustrations by John Mullin, Mullin Design Studio, Chesterton, Indiana

978-0-9860096-0-0

For information about purchasing additional copies of this book, visit
RetirementLifesGreatestAdventure.com

Printed in the U.S.A.

Dedication

To all my friends, acquaintances, working associates, and relatives who showed support and provided ideas for this book, and especially to my wife, Ann, who made timely suggestions and criticisms, proofread the contents and was continuously supportive of this book.

Credits

There were many people who contributed to my effort in writing this book. Many helped by letting me know how much they knew or didn't know about retirement. Some gave helpful suggestions. Some gave moral support. Some simply asked me questions.

My wife, Ann, was always supportive of my efforts in writing this book and my efforts to retire early. She even overcame her concerns about what it would be like to have me home all the time if I retired. She not only gave me ideas and made helpful suggestions, but she edited every page of this book.

Several people who worked with me had lunch with me frequently and discussed many of the important aspects of retirement. Among them are Armand Raponi, Ed Jakacki, Chuck Capperino, Jim Reicherts, Bill Swearengen and Bruce Swenson.

Others who helped in various ways include (in alphabetical order): Ray Acevedo, David Austgen, Bob Bottello, Linda Byall, Dick Cicenas, Bill Coggin, Don Diersen, Marie Dugan, Beth Fruin, Jeff Hibbard, Dave Hubinger, Bill Jones, Carolyn Marrouchi, Rick Oria, Bud Pulver, Armand Raponi, Peter Salvador, Leti Sanchez, Marty Shreiber, Dave Suban and Terry Supple.

Preface

Like my father before me, I always expected to retire at age 65 (conventional retirement age). For most of my working life, that's what I expected to do. Once a year, my employer sent me a statement that actually indicated my retirement date, which was April 30, 2006. That would have been my actual retirement date if I hadn't started thinking about whether I could retire sooner.

However, in my middle 50s, I discovered that my department manager preferred younger employees. I was passed over for promotions and raises became fewer and smaller. My situation led me to look at retirement options, which in turn led me to one of the best decisions I've ever made. A thorough review of my circumstances made me discover that, with a little planning, I could retire six years early.

Even with the prospect of early retirement, my difficult employment situation made me commit to a retirement plan that required that I stick it out for four more years. The four years were rough, but the experience forced me to think about early retirement and made me less emotionally connected to my employer.

Whether you retire early or not, there are certain considerations you must face. First, when you retire, you must face the fact that you have only a limited number of years to live. Depending on your health and family history, you might expect to live an average of only about 10-15 years at age 65. Thus, by retiring early, I may have added as much as 60% to my years of leisure. More importantly, in retiring at age 59, I was physically able to do nearly anything I wanted to do.

What that means is that the range of activities you can consider is almost endless. You are embarking on a grand new adventure where the sky's the limit. Furthermore, later in this book, you'll learn how early retirement can add years to your life. I have now been retired for over eleven years and have tried many of the things I recommend.

I dedicate this book to all the hard-working men and women who don't feel they are appreciated in their work. I hope this book will give you reason for hope. I hope that you can get away from an unhappy atmosphere and have more fun and inner satisfaction than you ever imagined possible.

Contents

Introduction

This book is not intended to give you a formula for a successful retirement. I don't intend to tell you what to do. Everyone is different and has different needs. No one can tell you what is best for you.

However, there is a lot of decision-making and planning involved with creating the ideal retirement for YOU. So, instead of suggesting what you should do, this book provides questions for you to ask yourself. Your answers to these questions will help you decide what you want to do with your retirement. Often you'll discover that you didn't even realize how many options you have. Also, you may discover that there are pitfalls to retirement that you never imagined existed.

Most of all, I hope to help you discover a whole world of opportunities that will make your life more fun, exciting, satisfying and fulfilling.

I have tried to become a living example of what many retirees want to be: Active, enthusiastic, involved, fit, healthy, happy and fulfilled. I have tried as many of the activities as I could, so I can recommend them with authority. Other activities have been suggested by the scores of retirees that I have interviewed for ideas. Also, I have experienced nearly every problem discussed in this book—either directly or indirectly. The information in this book involved 14 years of research. It could have been finished sooner, but investigating various activities and ideas often kept me from writing for months at a time. However, that is one of the benefits of this book—keeping busy. Often, being busy gives one a sense of purpose and happiness.

It is important for you to realize that life is what you make it. Traits such as honor, ethics, responsibility, and charity are in your nature or they aren't. It is up to you to search for them within you. If they are there, retirement is a time when you have the time and the opportunity to develop them.

Too often, a new retiree has no plan for spending his or her retirement years. Without a plan that includes enjoyable, exciting and fulfilling activities, a retiree can quickly lapse into inactivity. Inactivity is a dangerous state, since it affects us emotionally.

Too many retirees develop harmful drinking habits, or they overeat, or they fall into other bad habits. In combination with a lack of physical and mental activity, these habits can lead to boredom, becoming overweight, having poor health, and developing mental health problems, including depression and even Alsheimer's Disease. Very few people survive well in an environment of inactivity.

We're usually happier and healthier when we are busy. Certainly we deserve the rewards of retirement from a lifetime of work, but that doesn't mean we should become inactive. Retirement affords an opportunity to try new things—things that we *choose* to do. A variety of activities—challenging activities—that gives us satisfaction and self-fulfillment will provide a level of happiness that most of us cannot even imagine during our working lives.

Chapter One
Planning for Your Retirement

Why Should I Read This Book? Years ago, when I was in my twenties, I was given an assignment to research why men died within two years of retiring. I recall there was a statistic that about 50% of all men who retired at age 65 lived less than two years after retiring. I spent some time trying to find out why that was happening. I didn't find all the answers, but I did learn that two of the biggest reasons were psychological and physical. However, people live much longer now, but I am convinced that these factors influence life expectancy.

The psychological factors affected life expectancy because people who devoted their lives to their jobs were at such a loss when their work was taken away that they no longer had anything to live for. In other words, their work gave them purpose and value, and when they no longer had that, they simply gave up on life.

The other factor, physical, had to do with activity. Many men and women, who were active in their work, suddenly became inactive when they retired; that is, they lay around watching TV or reading or sleeping. Others, who had had desk-bound jobs, perhaps became too active too soon, playing golf, working on home projects, etc. In both cases the change in activity level at age 65 was too much for their bodies.

I recall that the statistics that indicated that many men died within just a few years of retiring also said that if you could survive the first two years, your life expectancy shot up to 20 years or so.

Thus, to me, I could choose to either live to age 65 or 66, or live to be about 85, depending on how prepared I was for retirement. I have now been retired for ten years, so it looks like I'll make my goal for the long haul. I want you to be able to do the same.

Preparing for Retirement

In my twenties I made the decision to do what I could to increase my life expectancy when I retired. I studied the factors that affect life expectancy. I researched everything I could about retirement and tried to prepare based on what I learned.

I learned that having challenging goals was important not only to your happiness, but also to your very mental health. I learned that the best goals were those you created long before you retired. The longer you have your goals, the more important they become to you.

For instance, I have been a skier since my twenties. I love snow skiing and I love competing. For most of my adult life, I have competed in amateur ski racing, generally the giant slalom. I have won some bronze medals and an occasional silver medal. All during my ski-racing years I had a major goal of winning a gold medal. I decided that when I retired I'd be able to spend more time getting in racing shape and spend more time racing, so I'd have a better chance to winning my first gold medal.

That was a major disappointment to me. I raced about forty times in the first two years after I retired and won only bronze medals and an occasional silver medal. Would I give up? No way! I decided that as long as I can ski, I'll exercise as much as I can to be in the best shape I can get into, and race with the hope that this will be the day. I thought I could win with the right ski and weather conditions, the right practice, the right conditioning, and a little luck. This hope kept me going and made racing exciting to me—and eventually it led to gold medals.

The physical aspect of ski racing provided a second benefit for me. It gave me a reason to go out and run, walk, bike ride, lift weights, stretch, and do all the other things that keep me in the best of shape. Without the physical goals, I'm not sure I'd have the discipline to keep going. So *having* a goal was more important than achieving the goal.

I concluded that if I want to be competitive at ski racing, I have to ramp up my conditioning. Thus, I decided to make my ski conditioning program a 365-day-a-year effort. This led me to a variety of physical fitness activities, including bicycle riding, speed walking, water volley-ball, basketball, ice skating and cross country skiing.

I have also developed lots of other goals, and all of them give me challenges that make life exciting for me. In each case, they motivate me to work hard to achieve them.

Bottom Line

So if you are planning to retire and are not sure whether you are really ready, or you are retired and sense that you are not getting as much out of life as you should, or if you want to explore all the possibilities of retirement, read on . . .

In this book, we'll explore many factors that affect your retirement:

Financial Considerations—Briefly, we'll help you decide if you are financially able to retire, whether or not you can retire early, and how you can figure out how much money you'll need. We'll discuss a little about investment principles and risk. We'll talk a little about the retirement options you may have at your workplace.

Psychological Considerations—We'll look into the effect that retiring from a long-term job (or a skill/profession that you have worked in for a lifetime) has on your feelings about yourself.

Emotional Considerations—We'll help you prepare for the emotional changes that occur when you go from your life's *work* to your life's *pleasure.*

Friendship—We'll discuss how to make new friends if most of your previous acquaintances were related to your work.

Spousal Relationship—Does spending a lot more time at home strain the relationship with your spouse? What can you do to help?

Health Considerations—How does retirement affect your health? How can you become more fit?

Activities—What kinds of activities can you consider for your leisure time?

Challenges—Why should you challenge yourself with lofty goals in your retirement?

Life's Greatest Adventure—How can retirement become life's greatest adventure and why?

"The One Thing"

People who are contemplating retirement spend a lot of time trying to decide what they will do with their time. Because retirement is so different from one's daily work and home schedule, the "new" life can be a little frightening. Many of my friends have put off retirement just because they couldn't see themselves enjoying it.

First, understand that you won't have as much leisure time as you expect. Most people slow down a little to "smell the roses." After I retired, I tended to sleep about a half-hour later than my "working" sleep schedule. Of course, when I worked I got up at 4:30 am to commute from northwest Indiana to Chicago for many years, so my idea of sleeping late will no doubt be different from yours.

Then I enjoyed the newspaper over a leisurely breakfast—a luxury that I had rarely experienced during my working years. I even did some of the puzzles in the paper. During my years of commuting from northwest Indiana to Chicago, I had rarely looked at more than the headlines. In the evening I usually went to bed before the evening news, so I was "out of it" most of the time.

Expect to be less efficient with your time. It is part of the adjustment process of going from a working attitude to a retired attitude.

Ideas for some of your major activities are shown in Chapters 12 and 13. I have tried to show as much variety as possible, based on the activities of friends and acquaintances. Also, I have tried many of the things listed. I tried to limit the ideas to those things that are valuable to an individual, that is, activities that will give you at least some self-satisfaction and fulfillment.

Also, I have tried to include some specialized or non-traditional activities that are more for those who are handicapped, those who have medical restrictions, and those with special situations, such as retirees who are single.

Much of this book is dedicated to the concept that to be truly happy, you must participate in major activities that keep you busy, challenge you and bring you self-satisfaction or fulfillment.

As you read through the lists of activities in Chapters 12 and 13, you'll find many that are of no interest to you but others that you'll want to try. My hope is that reading about some of these activities will generate new ideas for you. Also, retired people you know may recommend activities to you or suggest some activities are inappropriate. Take these suggestions from others with a grain of salt, since other people are not likely to know what is best for *you.*

Everyone is different, so the best ideas for investing *your* time will likely be new ideas that I haven't even thought of. People have asked me to recommend activities for them, but rather than tell you what to do, I want to give you ideas to help you decide what is best for *you.* It is important to understand that only *you* can decide what activity is truly fulfilling to you.

Remember the movie, "City Slickers" with Billy Crystal as "Mitch"? He asked "Curly," his cowboy mentor, what was really important in life. "Curly" told him it was just "one thing."

Mitch asked "What one thing?"

Curly told him that he had to find that out for himself.

So it is with you. Your "one thing" might be adopting a calf like in the movie—or maybe not. Most likely, it is something else—something that you will have to discover for yourself.

My "one thing" is challenging myself, both physically and mentally. Through sports, I push myself to see how much my middle-aged body is capable of. I am not a natural athlete, so this type of challenge is particularly difficult for me. By writing this book, and through other activities that I have participated in to help the community, I try to find out how much help I can provide to others. With other activities I challenge my mind.

When Should You Start Planning?

Start now! Ideally, you should start serious preparations for retirement about five years before you retire. Among the important things to do are making sure that your pension or IRA or savings are realistically sufficient to see you through your retirement years. Also, you are going to be more active, in most cases, so you should begin a fitness program that will reduce the physical shock of increased activity after you retire. Obviously, your financial resources will influence the kinds of activities you will choose.

Your attitude is important too. You should be looking forward to retirement—not to lying around doing nothing—but you should be looking forward to having the time to try new things. See the lists of possible activities in Chapters 12 and 13.

While most of the information in this book is written for those contemplating retirement about five years before they expect to retire, it is never too late to change your plans. I know many people who retired in a traditional way and spent their time watching TV, traveling or just lying around. If this describes you, please consider a more active retirement.

Sometimes a traumatic experience, such as fighting cancer or some other illness, or dealing with the loss of a spouse or friend, results in a major change in perspective.

For example, my wife thought she was in near perfect health and didn't have a care in the world until she was diagnosed with breast cancer. It was a terrible shock to her and changed her entire perspective about life. After going through various treatments and recovering her health over a year's time, she suddenly became concerned about her fitness. After learning that a high-level of fitness decreases your chances of a reoccurrence, she became an adherent to good health and fitness. She has become more active and vibrant, and considers the experience with cancer a sort of wake-up call. Also, she has become a support person for people dealing with the emotional aspects of dealing with cancer. She was even honored by the Red Ribbon Society (a cancer-fighting organization) for her efforts helping people deal with cancer.

Why Would You Want to Retire Earlier than Age 65?

During the time I researched the possibilities for early retirement and thought about what I would do if I retired, I discovered that I knew very little about retirement other than the fact that it takes a lot of money or a sizable pension. I knew little about what kinds of activities were available to me, what kinds of interests I would have, or even how I wanted to spend my time. In talking to others in my age group I discovered that most people knew even less about retirement than I did. Furthermore, I learned that some things are extremely important to know about, not only for happiness in retirement, but for survival itself.

The more I learned, the more issues I became aware of that I needed to address before or soon after I retired. For instance, how will my relationship with my spouse change when I'm at home two or three times as many hours a week as when I was working? Is there a psychological adjustment to be made when we stop doing the work that, for most of us, gave us a sense of purpose and value? Are leisure activities enough to keep us satisfied in retirement? Are there important physical health considerations to deal with when we go from a sedentary lifestyle to a more active retirement lifestyle? Why are some people afraid of retirement?

These are just a few of the questions that I found myself asking. I learned that answering, or at least being aware, of all these questions is important to a successful retirement.

In fact, answering these questions led me to learn that, if you are properly prepared, retirement is like a great adventure that can excite you every day for the rest of your life.

How to Adjust to Retirement

I had a very stressful job in a big company in Chicago. I commuted nearly 100 miles a day for decades. Between my daily tasks, phone calls, faxes, emails, voice mails, meetings and emergencies, I was stressed out at the end of every day. When I retired I was warned that it would be difficult to adjust to having a lot of leisure time.

The warnings were correct. After I retired, I found myself glancing at my watch every few minutes—even during breakfast. I kept waking up every morning at 4:30 am ready to go to work. I found it difficult to relax.

I did two simple things to overcome these work hangovers. First, I stopped wearing a watch. If I really needed to know the time, I wore a golf watch that hung from my belt. Every time I looked at my wrist, the lack of a wrist watch reminded me that I didn't really need to know what time it was. Also, a week after I retired, my wife and I took a week-long vacation to Maine and visited Acadia National Park. Being away from home helped to break the work habits, and the pleasant surroundings helped me learn to relax.

A movie I saw awhile ago, called "About Schmidt," contains some useful lessons about retirement. I urge you to rent this movie and watch it. The day after he retires, Schmidt goes back to work to see how his replacement is doing Schmidt's job. Everyone is happy to see him, but after several visits they considered him a nuisance. He soon realizes that they no longer want to see him.

This is a reality that you will have to face as a retiree. Your fellow workers were often your best friends too. They'll certainly miss you, but they don't have time to see you more than occasionally. *Get on with your life!* If you have other priorities, you won't have time to worry about what's going on at your former place of employment.

A few years after I retired, I went to a funeral of a guy I had worked with for 14 years. He was with a photography firm that I had worked quite closely with. Some of their photographers had known me for 33 years and I considered them friends. Each person I walked up to was friendly enough, but usually found a way to keep the conversations to just a few minutes— long enough to ask me what I was doing, but not long enough for me to go into detail. I noticed that they seemed to want to spend most of their time with *current clients.* And why not? These are people they see regularly and need to get along with. I'm from their past and am no longer relevant.

How Will I Spend My Time as a Retiree?

This is a question many would-be retirees ask themselves. The most naive ones will say that golf or fishing or something like that will be enough to keep them busy. Thoughtful people will realize that accomplishment leads to happiness and self-satisfaction. These thoughtful people usually don't have a clue about what they could do to achieve happiness and self-satisfaction. Unfortunately, these are the people who are afraid to retire and often put it off too long.

The most well prepared people have a specific game plan and are chomping at the bit to attack it as soon as they can retire. My goal with this book is to put you in this category.

Are You Ready to Retire?

Naturally, one must have financial resources to retire. It may be a pension, it may be a 401K, it may be Social Security, it may be a long-term savings plan or it may be a combination of these. It is not easy to determine how much it takes to be ready for retirement. It probably will require less than you think it will. A broader discussion of this problem will be discussed further in this book.

However, if you think you are financially prepared for retirement, how do you decide when you are emotionally and psychologically prepared to retire? A friend of mine had a very satisfying, if demanding, job in the government. He told me he thought he could afford to retire, but didn't know if he was ready for it. I told him, "When you get up in the morning, what is it that you would rather do? Go to work, or do something else?" If most mornings you'd rather do something else than work, then you are ready.

Try Several New Activities

What should you do when you retire? Many people are comfortable with activities that they have done before, and enjoyed. However, trying new activities is a little like trying new restaurants and foods. You may discover you like a food you haven't tried before; in fact, it might become your favorite food. You will never know if there is a food more to your liking, or a restaurant, or an activity, if you don't experiment. Even in my 60's I had discovered activities that I loved.

There is no "right" or "wrong" way to go about retirement. However, sometimes the things that seem most appropriate may lead to an unhappy ending. Here are a couple of stories about fictitious people that represent people I have known, and, I think, represent millions of retirees.

"Joe" was a blue-collar worker in a steel mill in northwest Indiana. He retired at age 65 after a hard work life. All Joe wanted to do was play golf, bowl, watch TV and drink a little beer. And that is what he did—literally. He believed that he had done all the work he needed to do in his life and now it was time to rest. Unfortunately, he became lazy, overweight and out-of-shape. Eventually, the golf and bowling became boring to him; instead, he watched more TV and drank more. At age 69 he developed liver problems and died after only four years of retirement.

"Al" was fortunate. He was able to retire a little early. At age 62 he had a small pension and Social Security. He was a college graduate and had had an office job. He wasn't particularly athletic, so he didn't take up any sports. His wife had passed away, so he had little companionship. He decided that reading would be a good use of his time. He created a strict regimen for his daily life. He got up every morning at 7 am, got dressed and went out to breakfast. Then he came back and read for a couple of hours. Following a light lunch, he went out to do errands (shopping, dry cleaners, bank, post office, etc.). He then read a little more, and then had his dinner. After dinner, he either read or watched TV.

After a few years, Al became bored with his lifestyle. However, instead of changing it, he continued with the same old rigid schedule. Eventually, he became depressed. This led to a feeling that the world was against him. He became angry and mean, and lived a miserable and sad life.

"Lynn" retired at age 65, but her pension was too little to live on. Even with Social Security benefits, she couldn't quite make ends meet. She ended up taking a low-paying service job with long hours. Although she had the energy to take up retirement activities, she didn't have the time to do anything but work and sit at home.

Even after 50 years as a teacher, "Wes" could think of nothing more fulfilling and interesting than to continue teaching. Also, he had a secret fear of retirement. He thought he would become bored and a bore. He was afraid of leisure. He had no idea of how he could spend his time as a retiree. As a result, he never discovered that he was really tired of teaching and never realized he had a hidden desire to travel and find exciting adventures to explore. He worked until the day he died.

What's the Solution?

All of these people had unhappy outcomes to their retirement plans. All of them had different situations, income levels, fitness levels, energy levels and interests. Thus, the solutions to their unhappy retirements would each be different from the other.

As a rule of thumb, they were missing something that could make their lives exciting and fulfilling. Instead of doing less, they might have been better off doing more. However, everyone is different, so everyone's idea of the ideal retirement is different. Also, most people don't think about what would be best for them. As a result, they may never discover the activities or lifestyle that would be ideal for them.

This book is intended to help you find out what would lead you to a happy, fulfilling retirement. It won't be easy. You will have to be willing to get out of your "safe zone"; that is, you will have to be willing to try new things, extend your interests, think "outside the box," create a personalized lifestyle, and search for activities that match your fitness level, health, energy, and financial situation. You may not be able to afford cruises or vacations to exotic parts of the world, but maybe you can find exciting things to do around where you live. If you can't get by on your retirement resources, maybe there is a new type of work you can do that is fulfilling, fun and financially rewarding. I teach at a university, sharing my professional skills with students who need them; one person I know substitute teaches, another person started a small business; still another person became a sports photographer.

The possibilities are endless. I hope that as you read on, you will begin comparing your interests, experiences, abilities and talents with possible activities that can turn your retirement into "life's greatest adventure."

Chapter Two

Emotional and Psychological Aspects of Retirement

Retirement means rest, relaxation, fun and games, right? You'll live a carefree life, right? Maybe not.

One of the unexpected aspects of retirement is the emotional let-down that occurs when you leave an employer for whom you've worked many years. Most people look forward to sleeping late, having more free time, being relieved of work stress, and retiring from the work you've done every day for the past 30-40 years.

Don't forget that some of your closest friends were working there with you. Some of them you'll still be able to see socially, but most either live too far away to see regularly, or they still go to work and just don't have the time to see you. A few months after retirement, many retirees feel a big let-down since they no longer see many of these former work friends. Some people have very few close friends outside of work.

You'll also miss some of the other positive aspects of your working life. If you have a responsible job or have employees working for you, after you retire you'll miss the power and respect that came with your job. Maybe you'll miss the excitement of going to work in the "city" every day, or the lunches at downtown restaurants, or the interesting and attractive people that you see on the street every day. You'll certainly miss the feeling of accomplishment that you got when you were paid for your hard work.

Many people I talked to are afraid to retire because of some of the changes they think will occur. Some retirees feel that they will have nothing to do after they retire. Some people are concerned that it will be more difficult to maintain a happy and healthy marital relationship when they suddenly began spending much more time with their spouses. These are legitimate concerns. See Chapter 9 for more about changes in married life and how to deal with them successfully.

Often your job, your skills, or your position entitles you to the pleasure of having the respect of others at work. Losing that respect as a result of retiring can be a big loss for you. One of my friends was the top guy in his field worldwide. Suddenly he wasn't even No. 1 in his own home. How do you deal with the loss of that kind of daily "high"?

There are also major problems concerning how you feel about yourself as a conscientious working person with a skill or trade or profession, versus how you feel as a retired, non-contributing person in your community. A discussion on how to deal with the loss of the sense of fulfillment you had from your work is provided later in this chapter.

Avoiding an Emotional Let-Down

After money concerns, the single biggest problem for the new retiree is the let-down resulting from how retirement changes how you feel about yourself.

One of my friends said he didn't want to retire from being a pharmacist and drug store manager. He mentioned not having enough money as one of his reasons. However, when it was suggested that he could work as much as he wanted as a part-time or vacation pharmacist, he admitted that there were other reasons. He really enjoyed seeing the customers, some of which he saw frequently. He enjoyed the responsibility he felt in caring for peoples' health and for the decisions he had to make in running the store. Ultimately, I agreed that to continue working might be best for him, although I regretted that he hadn't developed outside interests to take the place of his career.

The emotional changes that may result from retiring are rarely anticipated because people who experience them don't talk about them. As a result, the new retiree usually doesn't hear anything about this problem from other retirees. Nevertheless, these emotional changes are a very serious concern.

No matter what your job is, if you are conscientious about your work, your job gives you a feeling of satisfaction and accomplishment. Few people admit it, but nearly everyone enjoys some aspect of his or her job. It may be the feeling of accomplishment from doing a good job or making a great effort. It may be the joy of earning the respect of your fellow employees, subordinates or management. It may be the pride in the skills you have developed, the professional attitude you have, your leadership talents or your efficient demeanor.

However, what is most important is that you see yourself as a valuable, conscientious contributor to your employer, your business and the community as a whole.

You may not recognize this in yourself, or you may take it for granted, but nearly everyone feels the loss when it is gone. Its loss may leave you with an empty spot in your being, but it can also lead to more serious issues, such as depression. Depression is probably the most serious enemy of the retiree. So one of the first jobs of the new retiree is to find activities that replace the work they did that will provide the missing elements that make them feel good about themselves.

Taking Risks

One of the keys to having a successful retirement is to begin doing all the things you always thought you'd like to try. Most valuable of these activities are the ones that give you an intense feeling of satisfaction, whether it be from competing with others, earning income with your skills, or serving others by giving of your time.

However, many of these activities involve taking risks. Not risk of your life or health, but risk of your self-value. When you compete in work or play, you risk losing. Does losing hurt your feelings or self-esteem? When you go to your job, or do part-time work, or work with others in community service, do you find your ideas rejected by younger people? Do you sense that these people don't respect you because you are older? When you are interacting with others, do you notice that they have an attitude that they don't feel you are equal to them because you are older?

These are the risks you must accept when you start doing things you haven't done before. You must learn to deal with these risks. This process makes you a better, emotionally stronger person. It is part of what can give you satisfaction in your retirement. If you fail to deal with these risks, you will be damaged emotionally and you may withdraw into your shell. You have likely seen other older people do this. Be strong! Don't let others put you down.

Accept that many younger people are threatened by more experienced older people. They may try to suggest that your age and experience are undesirable. Take their attitude with a grain of salt.

In my working and professional life, I had a lot of success as a leader. I was respected for my leadership skills. So when I retired, I offered my leadership skills to help other organizations. Among these was a local ski club that seemed as if it could use some professional leadership. I had some success, but was tested by some younger leaders. These were typical young people. Smart but not experienced. We should all remember what we were like when we were in our 20s and 30s. We thought we knew everything; we certainly thought we knew more than "old people."

Now, as an "old person" (or do you prefer "senior"?), we will encounter people who are still "wet behind the ears." Now we know how it feels to know the answers but can't find people who want to listen to our wisdom.

All you can do is offer your advice, leadership, organizational skills and efforts. If they are rejected, it's not your problem. Don't let the rudeness of young people get you down. They are the ones who stand to lose if they don't take advantage of your valuable skills. I know this is hard to do because I went through it. You must politely accept the rudeness and criticism and then *back off.* You know the old saying: "You can lead a horse to water, but you can't make him drink." If they won't listen, go somewhere else to offer your services. If you are really strong, stick around and keep trying. Somewhere along the line someone may listen to something you suggest.

In any event, risk-taking is healthy. Understand that every new thing you try may involve some type of risk. How you handle it reveals the kind of person you are. The strong, self-reliant person can handle whatever comes along. It's part of self-development that keeps you growing as a person. You are never too old to grow.

Making Friends

Since many of your friends are people you worked with or are professional associates, an important task is to find new friends. As a retiree, some of your friends should be fellow retirees because these people have something in common with you. However, you should be open to all sorts and ages of friends. This makes you a more interesting person.

As an older person, it is not as easy to make friends as when you were younger. For one thing, there is the generation gap. Society has changed so much over the past 30 years that you may find you have little in common with those under 50 years of age. Computers, I-Pods, I-Pads, text messaging, streaming, Facebook, Twitter, Linked-In—these things and concepts may be beyond the understanding of many of us.

For others, they are things we just are not comfortable with. While I am familiar with all these concepts, and make use of some of them, I consider some of the social networking to be time-wasting and an imposition into a person's privacy. I can't imagine reporting everything I do on Twitter or Facebook.

As a result, you may find that you don't relate well enough to younger people to become friends with them.

Also, with decades of experience, wisdom and hindsight, often our opinions become stronger. I find that many people in my generation have such strong political, religious or moral views that they cannot communicate comfortably with many of their peers.

So, between generational issues, opinions, life experiences, marital status, lifestyle and economic status, you may find that there are few people you want to become friends with. However, they are out there; you just have to find them.

Another problem with making new friends is that people who you have known for decades have stronger ties to you than "new" friends. There is no substitute for "old" friends. This becomes especially obvious to people who move to a different part of the country after retirement. They complain that while there are new people, they often only become acquaintances. It takes a long time to make real friends. Several people I know have moved back to the areas where they spent most of their lives because they missed long-time friends and family. See Chapter 4 to help you decide whether moving to a better climate is best for you.

Attitude Is a Critical Part of a Successful Retirement

I mentioned in Chapter 1 that I thought psychological and physical issues can affect a person's life expectancy after retirement. Psychological preparation is just as important as physical conditioning in preparing for retirement. Psychological weaknesses can lead to serious emotional problems, such as depression.

I believe that depression is the biggest and most common obstacle in the way of a happy retirement. You'd be surprised how many people have faced this obstacle after retirement. Depression can be caused by many things, including stress, but to the retiree, depression is often associated with a lack of excitement in daily activities. Thus, the proper attitude can be a big factor in preventing depression and creating happiness. Somehow, you must develop a positive attitude about whatever activities you participate in.

That's why the lists of activities in Chapters 12 and 13 are so important. Most of the activities were chosen for the lists because they provide some form of satisfaction or self-fulfillment that can help a person defeat the onset of depression, and provide a feeling of satisfaction or self worth.

Many of us associate our self-value with our jobs. If I am a teacher, I associate my value as that contribution I make to the community. When I stop teaching, I begin to question my self-worth. If your job is answering the phone for a business, you see yourself an important cog in the communication done by that business. No matter what your job is—important or insignificant—you tend to see it as important in some way. Seeing our jobs as important is important to our self-confidence and self worth.

When you leave your job and stop getting a paycheck, you sometimes begin to question your self-value. That's a big reason why a retired person needs to find activities that generate feelings of self-worth and importance.

Naturally, if you spend time doing things you truly believe are important, then you have a better chance of developing a positive attitude about yourself. How you do that is up to you.

Reevaluating what is important to you is a good start. Spouses, children, other family members, and home should become more important to you. However, often the activities you participate in will become important symbols of your value to yourself. By selecting activities that do something for you or for others, it is easier for you to see that these activities are bringing happiness and fulfillment into your retirement life.

Passion or Obsession?

As I mentioned in Chapter 1, one of my major goals for the past 30 years was to win a gold medal in giant slalom ski racing. Over the years I have won many bronze medals and even a few silver medals, but never a gold. I believed that after retirement, I could spend more time on fitness and technique and increase my chances of winning a gold. In ski racing, your performance is adjusted for your age, that is, you get a time handicap based on your age and gender that makes it a little easier to perform well. As you get older, then, it is easier to win (assuming you maintain your fitness level). Since I retired, I have won a higher proportion of silver medal than before, and have gone from winning bronze and silver medals, to winning silver and gold.

I reasoned that, in order to raise my level of fitness, I had to take up off-season sports that would help me get in better condition all year round. I realized that as I get older it is harder to get in shape and stay in shape, and it takes a longer time to do it. Essentially, I must be in good shape all year round to be capable of performing in a demanding sport, such as skiing and ski racing, when winter comes.

A friend talked me into taking up bike riding. The muscles used for bike riding are strongly related to leg strength and stamina, which are also closely related to the requirements of skiing. The more bike riding I did, the better I skied. In order to push myself to higher levels of fitness, I began participating in organized bike rides. First, it was weekly 10-20 mile rides with my ski club, and then it was bicycle organization rides of 30-50 miles. Finally, I got involved in the "Hilly Hundred," a grueling 100-mile ride taking two days going up and down the hills around Bloomington, Indiana. This annual ride typically draws over 5,000 highly conditioned biking enthusiasts.

All these riding experiences were socially fun, physically demanding, and provided me with opportunities to reach high levels of fitness. Since I tend to be a little lazy, I welcomed the opportunity to ride with others and be influenced to keep going and not give up when I got a little tired.

I also looked for other fitness-related sports and activities. I regularly play basketball and water volleyball, and I like fast or speed walking. I work out regularly, bowl on a team, occasionally ice skate or cross-country ski, and participate in many other activities and sports.

Because of all these activities and sports, my wife thought I was a little obsessive. She said that I was getting carried away, first by the skiing, then by the bicycle riding and all the other athletic activities. She considers some of these sports to be extremely demanding and a little dangerous. I have repeatedly tried to explain that I like it that way. The effort required provides me with the satisfaction of accomplishment and a measure for improvement. That is, if I bike-ride 50 of the scheduled 100 miles in the "Hilly Hundred" one year and 65 the next, I can be proud of my improvement. The level of danger provides excitement, certainly not like sky diving or bungee-cord jumping, but still, dangerous enough that you have to take biking or skiing seriously in order to avoid injury.

Whether you call this obsession or a healthy passion for skiing and bike riding, I consider it healthy. Also, I'm convinced that this was a great way to put me in the position of being able to achieve my goal of "winning the gold." Best of all, it puts me far from the real danger of depression and a lack of enthusiasm about my interests.

Whether it is obsession or healthy passion, it does give you the drive to achieve valuable goals. And that is what is important. You need something to make you work hard to prepare your body to be able to rise to the challenges of physical goals. For most people, a well thought out fitness program will prepare them for whatever activities they choose, whether extreme or not.

I believe that being a little obsessive about several interests is really a good thing. At least it is good for me. My only problem is convincing my wife that what I'm doing is positive, not nuts!

By the way, three years after I retired I finally won my first gold medal in giant slalom. Hurrah!!

It's Not over Till It's Over

Most of us want to return to our former place of employment from time to time to see our former workmates. You may drop in for a visit; or you may go to lunch with some of the people you used to work with.

This is OK once in a while, but it can set you up for an emotional fall. When you've been away from your job for a while, you may find that your former friends and workmates don't really want to see you. Your interests have changed and no longer relate as closely with theirs. Also, things have likely changed at work, so you are no longer "in the loop."

As I mentioned in Chapter 1, the movie, "About Schmidt," illustrates the pitfalls of returning to your former place of employment too often. It is important to recognize that this part of your life is over.

It is important for you to move on from your attachments to your old job and fellow employees. If you continue to visit them too often, you will become a pain in the ass. Worse yet, you will eventually be rejected, and you will feel emotionally let down.

Changing Your Habits

One of the challenges you will face if you wish to have a rewarding, exciting and fulfilling retirement, is to avoid old habits. You can open yourself to more exciting activities if you are willing to try new things. You can teach yourself to be capable of changing your habits. A lot of the excitement in life is based on doing new things or doing old things in new ways.

Breaking old habits requires conscious effort. One way to do it is to deliberately do things in a different way than what you are used to. With practice you will welcome new things. However, it is not as easy as it seems.

Willingly accepting new ways of doing things leads to a willingness to try new things. That is the key to being comfortable trying new activities.

Challenging Yourself

Physical Challenges: I've always believed that most of us are physically capable of nearly anything if we are willing to try hard enough. As a retiree, I find it interesting to see just how physically strong I can become and whether I can increase my mental capabilities. With age, we are supposed to slow down both mentally and physically, but maybe that is not always the case.

I have surprised myself and met many goals that I thought were beyond my reach. Yet I try to take the attitude that I should try to make a full commitment to a goal and then see how close I can come to achieving it.

Now, as a retiree, I believe that I can achieve things that are normally the achievements of much younger people. Besides the pleasure and fulfillment you can win by achieving these goals, you are helping yourself physically and mentally.

Pushing yourself to your physical limits (when you are fit), helps you to learn more about the capabilities of your own body. You would be surprised how often you'll exceed your expectations. Bear in mind that higher goals of fitness require a more gradual improvement for older people. However, the effort may bear fruit as family members and friends may be surprised and impressed by your achievements.

For instance, on a "barefoot" cruise on a sailing ship, I challenged a young woman crew member, who had been a wrestler, to an arm-wrestling match. I didn't really plan to get involved in this, but once committed, I didn't want to back out. Undaunted by the chance of embarrassment of being beaten by a woman, I figured, "if she beats me, hey, what do you expect from a man over 60. On the other hand, if I win, that's a hoot!"

Well, I beat her! The match attracted so much attention from the passengers and crew that I eventually found myself in a match with our popular and robust captain. I went forward with the same philosophical attitude as with the woman crew member and won again. Although younger and tougher opponents and a tiring arm ended my string of victories, I was the hit of the evening because of my surprising ability.

And so it is; you never really know when your disciplined efforts can lead to fun and glory.

Mental Challenges: Pushing yourself mentally is equally rewarding and important to your health. Age often dulls the memory and sometimes leads to more serious mental problems. As nearly as I can tell, driving your brain in new directions and challenging your mental abilities will help your memory, your decisiveness and your mental clarity, as well as postpone or defeat mental problems, perhaps even Alzheimer's disease. Certainly these things can be thought of as mental exercise.

Here are some ways to do mental exercise:

➤ Teaching at a local college or school.

➤ Writing anything.

➤ Playing thinking games, such as Sudoku, crossword puzzles, etc.

➤ Playing competitive board games, such as chess, checkers, Monopoly, etc.

➤ Playing sports that include a challenge to the mind, such as ping pong, golf, etc.

➤ Taking a class to learn something.

No one has ever told me that challenging your brain is bad for your mental health.

I don't know if it is true or not, but at 70 years old, I believe my brain is just fine. However, with age, our memories become less agile. I feel like my mind is like a four-year-old computer with only one kilobyte of memory left. It seems that if I learn something new today, I have to forget or erase something from my memory. It's funny, but it might be true.

Chapter Three

Just Say "No!"

Since I retired, I have learned that one of this country's greatest natural resources is the retiree.

It seemed as if every organization I belonged to suddenly thought I would make a great leader, or they really needed my expertise. In no time I was busy every day doing different things for various organizations. In addition, I was looking for enjoyable, satisfying, exciting and/or fulfilling activities to participate in.

After a while my wife pointed out that I was busier than I had been while I was working. I had made two mistakes.

The first was that every time I found something I liked doing I would add it to the activities I did regularly. Over a year or two I went from a few activities to scores. The second error was getting involved in too great an extent in too many organizations.

I guess I thought that, as a retiree, I had an unlimited amount of time available. Also, I didn't recognize that working people who were leaders in various community, religious, alumni, sports and dozens of other types of organizations were constantly looking for help. Working people believed (and were somewhat correct in believing) that most retired people have time on their hands.

Eventually, my wife suggested that I should drop something for every new thing I add. That turned out to be good advice.

Be Selective

Once you are aware that many people and organizations will want you to work for them for *free,* you are in a better position to judge where you want to spend your time. It is good for you in many ways to be involved in organizations, and there are many benefits for you in doing this. You get a feeling of satisfaction from being involved, and most organizations will show appreciation in some way. Also, as indicated in Chapter 2, it is emotionally good for you do donate your time in useful and important activity.

However, if you try a lot of new activities, you will find that your "dance card" will fill up quickly. What's good about that is that you can pick and choose which, of the many good ways to spend your time, is best for you. Think about each opportunity you have. Is it valuable to the organization that is asking for your time? Is there some value to you? That is, do you feel some satisfaction from your efforts?

I know of some people who donate their time to organizations, but they are taken for granted. I was once told that anything that is free is worthless to the recipient. I wrote and published a book for my employer some years ago. The company wanted to break even on the cost of the book by selling copies at cost. Our cost was about $12, so we sold the book for $15 to cover the book's cost and shipping and handling. We thought it was a very useful book, but sales weren't as good as we hoped. Eventually, a bookstore that sold our book told me that our book sold for half the price of a similar book that wasn't nearly as good. However, when people compared the books, they assumed that the more expensive book was better. When we raised the price, we sold more copies.

The same is true with you. There is a danger that if you do something for free, those who you are doing it for may value your efforts at too low a level. If they don't recognize the value of your contribution, stop doing it.

In some cases, paying you a nominal amount of money enhances the value the organization puts on your efforts. I do some teaching at a local university as an "adjunct professor." I have learned that this pays about one-tenth to one-fifteenth the amount that a full professor gets paid. However, the fact that they pay me anything forces them to consider my value.

I have had a large number of part-time jobs since I retired. Some were consulting jobs in my industry doing what I had done before retirement. These generally paid well. Other jobs were consulting in other related types of work. I was disappointed to learn that these usually paid one-third of what I expected. I had to revise my thinking. Most of this work required less effort that I had made before retirement, entailed less responsibility, and needed less professional training. I learned to enjoy the part-time work without worrying how much I was getting paid.

Part-time paying work or volunteering for charitable or non-profit organizations is not about hard work, promotions and advancing pay scale. It is about enjoying yourself doing something rewarding for you and useful for someone else.

If someone asks you to do something, compare all the factors. How valuable is what you are doing to the organization you are doing it for? Is the value to them worth the effort for you? What are you getting out of it? Satisfaction? Pay? Enjoyment? Fulfillment? Don't do it only because you are bored. Find other types of activity to replace boredom. If it isn't worth your time and effort, just say "no."

Chapter Four
Where Will You Live?

The first thing my wife and I talked about after I retired was where we should move to for our retirement. We discussed many different geographic areas that attract retirees. We discussed areas where we currently had friends living. We discussed climates. We also discussed the economics of moving to a new home.

We were living in the Chicago area (actually northwest Indiana, about 40 miles from downtown Chicago), so the climate can be severe, especially in winter. We had friends calling us from Florida and Texas when we had a foot of snow on the ground and the temperature was below zero. They invited us to visit them, in places where it was warm and sunny. Sometimes they made fun of us for living in an undesirable climate.

On the other hand, we both like to snow ski, so moving farther away from the snow was not necessarily a priority for us.

Ultimately, we decided to stay where we were. However, six years after I retired, we decided to move into a newer home about ten miles away. This home had significantly lower maintenance, and a much smaller yard to mow and tend. Our reasons for staying in northwest Indiana might not be appropriate for you, but they are reasons you should be aware of. Sometimes there are less obvious factors you should consider.

The biggest factor was *friends.* We have many friends living in the area where we live now, and moving would make it difficult to maintain these friendships. I emphasize this in many places in this book, but one of the biggest factors in a happy retirement is interaction with people. Without friends, life can become lonely, especially for those who are living alone.

However, after you retire, it is more important than ever to remain connected with friends or to develop strong friendships. Some of us have lifelong friends we want to stay close to. Some people have the fortunate ability to quickly form friendships. If you are among these lucky people, you can move anywhere and develop friendships quickly. You can move anywhere and be happy.

You may also have friends in another parts of the United States, or in other countries. What if you move somewhere to be near a good friend and that good friend moves somewhere else? Will you move too? What if the friend you live near passes away? People have many reasons to move: Health, family, affordability, etc. You might make a commitment to move and then buy property, only to find your friend has to move somewhere else. This is something to think about.

Also, you usually expect to make friends in a new area you move to. Maybe you will, but *old* friends are always truer than *new* friends. Often, the people you meet in a new location are simply acquaintances, not real friends. For most people, friendship is a long process that can't be rushed. And why give up friends you have nurtured for years to find new friends that may or may not exist where you move to?

As to climate, we like warm weather sometimes and snowy weather other times. Ultimately we addressed the question of: Where do you go on vacation when you already live in the perfect place? That is, what if you already live in Florida, Texas or Arizona? You are living in a vacation wonderland. Where do you go on vacation then? More and more of our acquaintances are realizing that it is easier to plan a trip to visit friends or enjoy a warm climate than it is to move your home. Staying put can be ideal—the advantages of living near friends and family, yet the opportunity to go somewhere else when you feel like it.

I'll admit that as the years go by, I like tending the lawn and shoveling snow less and less. Also, when it snows for several days in a row, I get really tired of winter. However, then a beautiful spring comes along, and I remember why I stayed in the north.

However, there are lots of other considerations. For example, do you have children and grandchildren you want to be geographically close to? Will you follow them if they are forced to move to another area because of job or other developments? Are you comfortable visiting children and grandchildren just a few times a year? These are important issues to think about when making a decision to move.

What about other family members? Do you have a parent or sibling who is dependent on you living nearby? Are there any others whose welfare or happiness is impacted by your proximity to them? Are family pets a consideration? Some pets are traumatized by changing geographic relocations.

Depending on how important family, high school, college and workmate reunions are to you, you should take their locations into consideration. Living in areas near where you were born, or went to school, or worked, can make visits to reunions easier and less costly.

Naturally, there are economic considerations concerning your choice about where you will live. Usually, desirable retirement areas and near-perfect climates require a greater cost commitment. Most of us can't sharply increase our living costs in order to live in "paradise."

Spending a little time thinking and planning may help you avoid making decisions that you will regret later. Remember, once you retire, it is usually more difficult and expensive to correct financial mistakes.

It is common knowledge that retirees have accumulated much wisdom during their lives. You know how to think things out and weigh the pros and cons of many factors. Make use of all that wisdom and make decisions that do you credit. Show those young Turks that you are smarter than they give you credit for.

Also, "paradise" may be subject to problems you don't currently have. Florida has hurricanes; California has earthquakes and tropical storms; and Arizona has droughts. No place is perfect; make sure you move to get away from one problem and then experience new ones.

Chapter Five

Friends

Most retirees give very little thought about how retirement affects the make-up of their circles of friends. Typically, for a working person, a large proportion of your friends are the people you work with, followed by neighbors, members of organizations and teams you are involved in, and long-time friends. Often, work demands leave little time to cultivate many additional friendships.

After we retire, we suddenly realize that we won't see many of our work friends regularly. Other friends and neighbors may still be in the work force and thus we will not see them during the day. If you retire at age 65, many of your acquaintances will already be retired. It will be easy to continue and grow those relationships. However, if you retire early, say at age 59, you'll find that your friends are still working. Even socializing with friends on weekday nights is a problem since most people who work have to go to bed early for work the next day. You may even find that friends who are still working will avoid you. They may be jealous of your retirement status. They may believe they have less in common with you than they did before. They may simply not have time to associate with "retirees" because they believe you'll waste their time with idle chatter.

This friendship problem can become a major cause of boredom and depression. You may have no one to hang out with anymore.

Obviously, you can't go back to your former place of employment very often. Besides getting in the way, you'll find that many of your former acquaintances no longer have much in common with you. They may even resent the fact that you are retired since they aren't. It is critically important to find some new friends. It is time to move on!

Part of my weekly regimen is to run/walk through my neighborhood or in a local park. During the course of my walks, I have had great opportunities to meet people. I met perhaps 20 neighbors during my neighborhood walks, and a half dozen people who have walking/running in common with me when I walked though parks.

Also, I take advantage of having more leisure time to be able to spend more time outdoors, and sometimes I meet people who just happen along. Those of us who worked in offices, factories or other indoor environments will especially appreciate the opportunity to spend more time outdoors.

Retirement has also given me more time to spend in organizations of interest to me, such as a ski club, a bowling league, a high school alumni association and a college alumni association. These organizations have provided an excellent way to get to know people and make new friends. Finally, the company that I retired from has several retirement organizations that meet for lunch or other activities. Here, I find I have much in common with the retired people who worked with me or in different departments of the same employer.

At these retirement luncheons or other activities, we can talk about old times, or changes in the company, or discuss new products or developments of our former employer. Often we talk about the financial situation of our former employer, or our own finances. Since most of us own some stock or are part of a retirement plan, we have much in common, and have enjoyable and stimulating conversations.

When you read Chapters 12 and 13, you will find many activities that afford the opportunity to meet new people and make new friends. When you are participating in activities with others, you soon realize that you have that activity in common with them. If they are retirees, you will find that you have a lot in common with the others doing the same things you are doing.

Plan before you retire—rekindle old relationships, seek out and befriend old classmates, etc. Look for people getting ready to retire. As you get older, you really will appreciate the treasure that good friends provide to you. It is well worth the effort to reestablish friendships with former friends and search for new friends you have common interests with. You won't succeed with every effort to make a friend, but the friends you establish relationships with will provide you with much enjoyment and companionship.

Also, Chapter 4, "Where Will You Live," gives some insight as to how moving to a new location, climate or different part of the country affects your circle of friends and acquaintances, and opportunities for making new friends. And don't forget family. Retirement may give you the time and opportunity to improve relationships with siblings, cousins, nephews, nieces and more distant relatives.

Chapter Six

Is Work Unhealthy for You?

You probably already know that you must improve your fitness level if you plan an active retirement. However, besides getting in shape for the increased activity of retirement, you would be well advised to think about your general health. Retirement can have a dramatic effect on your overall health. Physical fitness and robust health go hand-in-hand with getting the most out of retirement. Many people wait too long to retire and then develop health problems that put a serious crimp in their enjoyment of retirement activities. On the other hand, sometimes your health will improve dramatically after retirement. That brings me to the story of Bob M., a guy I worked with in Chicago.

While I was editor of an industrial magazine, Bob was my production manager. That is, in addition to producing hundreds of pieces of literature for other departments, he also arranged printing for my magazine. Dozens of people were after him all the time, trying to get their jobs printed as soon as possible. A rule in production is that everyone tries to make up for their slow work in writing, editing, and design by pressuring the production manager to make up for their lateness. Bob was in a frazzle all the time.

Besides all this stress, he had a problem with cholesterol. In his forties he had quadruple by-pass surgery and barely survived. Then, over the next twenty years, he had numerous angioplasties. Finally, in his late fifties, he had another quadruple by-pass surgery. He once told me all he had to do was look at rich food and his cholesterol would go up 50 points.

One day he told me he was going to retire early (at age 62). He felt that, with all his health problems, he couldn't expect a long and happy life, so he wanted to get some joy out of life while he still could. I remember he told me he was going on a vacation to Florida soon after retirement. I suggested some interesting attractions to visit along the way, but he said he wanted to get there in two days. "Why?" I asked. "Shouldn't you take your time and enjoy the trip? After all, you're retired now and shouldn't be in a hurry."

Bob agreed. He hadn't thought about the fact that he no longer had to hurry. He was so used to doing everything at work on an ASAP (as soon as possible) basis that it never occurred to him that he no longer needed to hurry. I hoped that our conversation would make him realize that he could now slow down ". . . and smell the roses."

Anyway, a couple of years later Bob called me and asked if my wife and I would be interested in meeting him for dinner. Although we both lived in the Chicago area, Bob and his wife lived in a southwest suburb and I lived in northwest Indiana, 30-40 miles away. He suggested meeting in a restaurant halfway. I thought that was a good idea and suggested a great steak place in about the right area. However, I said, "We could meet at this great steak place, but with your concerns about cholesterol, that might not be acceptable to you."

"No problem," he said. "I love steak."

When we met, I was shocked at his appearance. He looked 5-10 years younger than the last time I had seen him. He seemed more energetic too.

"Boy, retirement must really agree with you," I said.

"Well, after I retired I realized that a lot of my health problems were a result of stress on the job," Bob said. "I'm much more relaxed now, and don't have much stress in my life. My cholesterol is also much easier to control now, and I can eat a lot of foods that I couldn't consider eating before. I can even eat steak!"

I realized then that stress can be a serious health issue for many people. Obviously, most jobs don't create high levels of stress. For people in those jobs, stress is a non-issue. Also, some people teach themselves to deal with stress in a healthy way so it doesn't have a harmful effect on their health. During my last ten years of work, I went to a fitness center three times a week at lunchtime. A midday workout seemed to lower my stress level significantly. Also, I taught myself to not let work problems that were beyond my control upset me.

41

However, there are some people who just cannot deal effectively with stress. Those people should avoid stressful jobs. Even if the job pays well (and high-paying jobs seem always to be stressful), you should weigh your health against the financial rewards of the job. In Bob's case, there were many people who continuously put him in a stressful mode. For him, to control stress was nearly impossible.

Those who choose to work in a stressful environment should consider early retirement. As you get into your late forties and fifties, high levels of stress can negatively affect your health and even kill you. Although I don't think the medical community has proof, it seems likely that high stress is related to heart conditions, cancer, nerve problems and dozens of other ailments. I believe stress also contributes to depression and other mental ailments, and can cause nerve and muscle problems, such as a stiff neck and shoulders.

If you are a person in a high-stress job and you are not good at dealing with stress, you may end up like Bob. The good news is that retirement may serve as a youth elixir. You may gradually find that you look and feel younger, and that your health has improved dramatically.

Dealing with Stress

As a matter of fact, I had stress issues too, but I had them earlier in life. My first significant promotion came at a time when I had a lot of personal problems, including a death in the family.

I was a nervous guy anyway, but suddenly I had issues that raised my stress level to mountainous heights. At age 33, people were telling me that I would have a heart attack by the time I was 40.

Well, I didn't have a heart attack, but I developed serious stomach problems. At one point I was doubled up with pain for hours at a time. When I saw a doctor, he said that I would have to take stomach relaxing pills for the rest of my life or I would develop ulcers. He also put me on a permanent diet that basically eliminated everything that tasted good to me.

I couldn't accept that kind of life, so I addressed the causes of my problem. I realized that stress and nervousness were not problems caused by others, but were problems caused by me. When problems occurred, I could choose to get upset over them, or I could choose to take them in stride.

Essentially, I decided that, when disaster struck, that I could choose one of two courses of action. I could worry myself to death or I could attack the problem. What I figured out was that some problems couldn't be solved and some could.

For instance, part of my job involved visiting buildings around the country and having a photographer take pictures of them. The problem was that the pictures only looked good when taken on a sunny day. Cloudiness or rain or snow prevented us from getting our job done. All the travel and cost was wasted, and I failed to do my job.

What could I do? The answer: Nothing! This is a situation where worry is of no value and there is no action that will change the outcome.

On the other hand, what if my stress was caused by my being late for a writing deadline? I could worry all night, or I could get to work and work all night if necessary. While working all night is certainly not fun, I discovered I could channel the nervous energy into making a successful effort.

Dealing with stress is a lot more difficult than is seems. Often a situation occurs so suddenly that you are stressed out before you know it. Thus, you must develop a habit of identifying stressful situations instantly and deciding what action to take or deciding there is no action appropriate. It takes time and effort to develop this habit, but with time and effort, anyone can do it.

There is a saying I sometimes use to remind me to decide whether an action or inaction is the most appropriate solution. It goes like this:

"Grant me the serenity to accept the things I cannot change, the courage to change the things I can, and the intelligence to tell the difference."

Channeling Nervousness into Productive Power

After I developed the habit necessary to deal with stressful situations without harming myself, I discovered that nervous energy can be tapped to provide a source of power. This works really well for something like public speaking. Everyone is frightened by public speaking. Even seasoned speakers get nervous when they are about to address an audience. But it is possible to channel that nervousness into power. In the case of speaking, you can channel it into a powerful voice.

Athletes are familiar with this concept. People are nervous before a big game. By concentrating on channeling their nervous energy, they can use it to enhance their performance.

In nearly all cases, when you become experienced with channeling energy, you feel nervous until the beginning of your speech, athletic performance, or whatever. However, as soon as you start, the nervousness disappears and your performance is improved.

As a retiree, you still will have stressful situations to deal with, you still will be nervous about doing new things, such as appearing before a group or making a mistake. However, you now have the tools to keep these things from hurting you. You can be the wise elder that people expect you to be.

Fitness for Retirement

Fitness is important for those contemplating retirement. Many of us, because of the nature of our jobs, don't have the time, opportunity or inclination to keep ourselves fit. Many of us have sedentary jobs that keep us sitting down most of the day. Also, we are often too tired from working to want to spend much time exercising or being active after a day at work. Unfortunately, many of us believe that we are reasonable fit, when we really are not.

For a happy, active retirement, we will need to get into shape. The increased activity of an adventurous retirement can have unfortunate results if we are not physically prepared.

A few years before I retired I decided to join a fitness center near my office. I figured I would tune myself up a bit. Because of my advanced age, I had to take a stress test to make sure I was fit enough to get fit. I was realistic enough to realize I wasn't in excellent shape, but I expected to be at least average. I was in for a surprise. I was well *below* average in fitness.

I attended the fitness center as often as possible (at least twice a week) for the ten years before I retired. Thus I was physically prepared for retirement.

However, after I retired, I became lazy and unmotivated. I hated the work it took to improve my level of fitness or even to stay in shape. So I searched for things that I could do that would either increase my level of fitness without feeling like work, or I found ways to motivate myself.

For instance, I became involved in activities that required a high level of fitness, such as snow skiing, bike riding, fast walking, etc. As I improved my skiing ability I discovered that amateur giant slalom ski racing motivated me to get in better and better shape. To be good at these athletic activities required a long-term commitment. In fact, for ski racing I had to maintain a high level of fitness year round.

So, when I don't think I have the energy or motivation to exercise, I simply think about how what I do today will allow me to enjoy doing something six months from now. Curiously, the stronger I feel physically, and the better my body looks, the more I feel motivated to be even better.

Chapter Seven

Lump Sum versus Annuity

There are many different ways that a retiree receives a pension. Employees may be paid a "lump sum" or a traditional pension (a monthly annuity). Social Security has various payment options beginning at age 62. Most people also have savings plans, 401K* retirement plans, IRAs (Individual Retirement Accounts), etc.

More and more employers are offering employees the option of retiring with a lump sum instead of a traditional pension. There are many advantages to receiving a lump sum, but there are also some scary disadvantages.

Traditional pensions have been paid as an annuity, that is, monthly payments for the life of the retired employee. When the employee dies, the pension ends. Some employers offer an option that permits the employee's spouse to receive a portion of the annuity payments after the employee dies. However, most plans that permit the spouse to receive a portion of the annuity after the employee's death also will reduce the size of the employee's monthly annuity payment while the employee is alive. Keep in mind that the annuity is basically a monthly payout of a specific amount set aside by the employer for the employee's benefit.

For instance, if the employee selects the traditional monthly annuity payout and that payout is $2,000 per month, you may expect it to be reduced to say, $1,500 per month, if the employee selects an option whereby the spouse is to receive $1,000 per month after the retired employee's death.

---

*401Ks are investment plans created by federal law. They permit employers to invest money from your paycheck into investments of your choosing (usually) from an assortment they recommend. Sometimes the employer matches the employee's contributions to some degree. Also, usually the employer has the employee invest before-tax dollars, that is, money you haven't yet paid taxes on. Generally, the employee converts the 401K to an IRA (Individual Retirement Account) at retirement and pay taxes on withdrawals when they are made.

The disadvantages to the annuity payout are the following:

1. The payout is usually based on a relatively conservative interest rate, likely lower than you would get yourself if you shopped around.

2. Under certain circumstances in which your employer goes into bankruptcy or in the case of a corporate takeover, it is possible to lose part or all of the pension.

3. When you and your spouse die, there is no remaining sum to be left to your children.

On the other hand, you won't lose your pension if the economy turns bad. The monthly payout is usually calculated prior to your retirement, so you always know that you are getting a check, and you can plan your finances based on knowing you will receive the same amount each month. If you enjoy the comfort of a regular paycheck while you are working, you may also feel more comfortable receiving a regular (and predictable) pension check.

Lump Sum Payouts

There is more work (and risk) involved with looking after a lump-sum payout. When you choose to take a lump-sum payout at retirement, you become responsible for taking care of the money. You will have to make decisions to invest it wisely, but you must also plan your investments so you can provide your own paycheck.

Periodically (once a month or once every couple of months), you have to cash something in or withdraw money from one of your investments and deposit it into your checking account, much like a paycheck. This activity requires you to remember to move money into an account that makes it immediately available. It also requires you to make decisions on which account or investment to take the money from, depending on the performance of the investment or interest rates. All this can become pretty tedious after a few years.

Since you are receiving a lump sum in one big payment, you must invest it to earn additional income. You will want to create an Individual Retirement Account (IRA). Otherwise, you will have to pay income tax on the entire amount in the year you retire. If you set up an IRA, you have to pay income tax only on the amount you withdraw each year. Most financial advisors recommend that you try to live off the income your lump sum earns, rather than the principal (more about this later).

When you receive your lump-sum payout, you must be aware of how much of it is before-tax income and how much is after-tax income. If your employer had allowed you to invest a part of your income as a "before-tax" investment, then this money becomes taxable when you retire. On the other hand, if it is an "after-tax" investment, that means you have already paid tax on it and will not have to include that part of your payment in your tax considerations. Normally, your employer will refund the "after-tax" portion of your investment as a separate check, so that it is clear that you do not have to pay taxes on it.

To determine the amount of your lump-sum pension, your employer generally calculates the amount of money that would be used to generate the monthly pension payout, and adjusts that amount based on an economic indicator, such as current Treasury bond rates. Then, your employer creates two checks, one check for the amount of money you have already paid into your pension account that you have paid taxes on and another for the amount that is fully taxable (that your employer paid into the account and that taxes have not yet been paid on). Note that depending on your situation and employer, you may have a contributory pension account where the portion that you have paid in after taxes, is not taxable. Some pension accounts are paid for entirely by your employer; in these cases, 100% of your pension account is taxable.

Individual Retirement Accounts (IRAs)

Typically, the retired employee will take the taxable lump-sum check and roll it over into an Individual Retirement Account (IRA) to avoid paying taxes on the whole amount immediately. If the check is made out to an "IRA custodian," such as a broker, financial planner, bank, etc., then you don't have to pay any taxes until you withdraw funds from the IRA. To do this, you must have your employer make out the lump sum check to the IRA custodian "for the benefit of" (FBO) yourself.

There are complex rules concerning how to do this and the process of withdrawing funds. We will not go into those complexities here. There are many sources for this information. You'll need to consult with a tax advisor, your bank, your broker, your financial planner or your employer to learn the current rules and procedures. However, in general, you are allowed to withdraw funds from your IRA to live on periodically, beginning at age 59-1/2. The advantage of setting up an IRA, rather than just depositing the lump sum into your savings account, is that you can earn interest, dividends and capital gains on the total lump sum if you have an IRA and pay taxes only on the withdrawals. If you deposit the lump sum into your savings account (that is not an IRA), you'll pay up to one-third of it in taxes. Obviously, you can't earn as much by investing two-thirds of the amount as you can investing the whole amount.

Another requirement that you should be aware of is that you are required to withdraw a portion of your IRA beginning when you reach the age of 70½. The rules for how much you have to withdraw depend on your age and how much money you have in your IRA.

However, when you invest in an IRA, keep in mind that you don't pay taxes on the income it generates, but you also can't write off losses from downturns in the stock market. This, of course, prevents you from using losses to reduce your taxes. On the other hand, you will eventually pay taxes on the principal amount and any income it generates. In this situation it is very important that the investments you make are safe or conservative, so that your risk of losing money is small.

Another alternative to consider is to put all or some of your retirement funds into a Roth IRA. This is a sort of "after tax" IRA. Rather than paying taxes on the portion of your IRA that you withdraw each year, you pay taxes on the entire amount of your IRA, and then convert it to a Roth IRA. In this type of IRA you don't have to pay any more tax on the remaining amount or any income it generates.

Don't Blow It!

The big problem with taking your pension as a lump sum is that you become personally responsible for investing it and conserving your lump-sum pension. If you make a bad investment decision or are irresponsible about conserving the money, you can easily lose much or all of it. The problem, then, is that you are retired and can't start over. Losing it is a "fatal error."

In fact, you won't even want to spend any of the lump-sum principal. You have to invest it in a way that permits you to live off the income it generates. If you spend as little as 5% of the principal, you'll find that you have to increase the percentage of the principal you remove each year *and* increase the amount to keep up with inflation. There's a good chance you'll go through the whole thing in ten years or less.

You are going to have to take a long sober look at yourself. Are you responsible enough to make conservative investments and live only on the income they generate? Are you disciplined enough to invest in conservative, safe investments, when your friends are telling you about all the high-profit investments they know about? A rule of thumb is that you can't believe the amounts of losses or gains your friends tell you about. It's like going to a casino—some people don't want to admit their losses, so they tell you they won. Others will brag about their winnings and exaggerate them.

If you are not confident in your ability to take care of this large sum of money, take the annuity. In total dollars, there's not much difference between the amounts you will receive from investments compared to an annuity, and it's much safer. As I said before, the big disadvantage with an annuity is that there may be no capital to pass on to your children. On the other hand, a few small mistakes with a lump sum and you'll not only have no capital to pass on to your kids, but you'll have to borrow from them to get though your retirement years.

If you decide you can be trusted with a lump sum, do not trust yourself to decide how to invest it. You would be amazed at how many good-sounding investments are really bad investments. For many years, I invested most of my 401K* money in my company's stock. My company was one of the best "blue-chip stocks" available. They hadn't failed to pay a dividend in something like 50 years. The stock had split and doubled several times. And I was in a position to know my company was well managed.

Ultimately, another company tried to take over my company because my company was so successful. Although they failed, the aftermath resulted in the stock going from about $50 a share to about 12 cents. I lost well over $100,000. Later, I read some investment advice that suggested you should never invest more that 10% of your capital in your own company. The reason? It is nearly impossible for a person to make unbiased decisions about a company he or she is emotionally involved with. Well, I know now.

Unless your job is investing other people's money, you can't trust yourself to invest your own money when you are depending on it for life itself. Don't take a chance. Hire an advisor. Financial advisors are not perfect, but they are a damn sight more able to protect your investments than you are.

There are many kinds of advisors. Banks, stockbrokers, mutual funds, insurance companies, financial advisors, financial planners, etc., all want to help you invest your money. Some of them charge hefty fees. A common fee of 1½% or 2% amounts to $7,500 to $10,000 on a principal of $500,000. However, you can expect a return on your investments that is greater than that fee plus what you might be able to earn from your own expertise.

Sometimes, if you have a lot of money, your bank, stockbroker or insurance company will give you advice free of charge. However, it seems as if every one of them has his or her own portfolio to promote. Insurance companies will want you to put at least part of your investment into insurance, an annuity or some other product they sell. Banks will push for CDs (certificates of deposit) or other products they sell. Stockbrokers and advisors often have a specific portfolio of products they prefer to deal with.

What you want is someone who wants you to invest in what is best for you, regardless of what is best for them. In other words you want someone that just sells you investment advice.

You'll have to interview several potential advisors. *This is important!* If you screw this one up, you can also lose some or all of your money. Be serious about these interviews. At the end of this chapter are some suggestions for questions you can ask that will help you choose the right advisor for you. Basically, you're looking for someone who is interested in understanding your financial goals and risk comfort level, that is, how conservative are you about your investments and what kinds of investments are you willing to make. One problem with a lot of advisors is that they get a fee or kickback from some mutual funds they invest your money it. Usually this is true with "front-end loaded" mutual funds. You pay a hefty fee to invest in the mutual fund and some of the fee goes back to your advisor.

When an advisor recommends a lot of "front-end loaded" mutual funds, that's a tip off that he or she may not have your best interests in mind. Don't get me wrong, some front-end loaded mutual funds are a good deal and are well worth investing in. However, as a rule of thumb, you can do just as well with mutual funds that have no investment fees (or have small annual fees). Advisors that look to make money on you from both the annual fee you pay them and fees from mutual funds you invest in will recommend making frequent changes in your investment portfolio**. They may do this because every time they make a change they get another fee from the front-end loaded mutual fund. This activity is known as "churning," that is, churning your account or moving your money around between different investments to maximize their income (in fees) from it.

The arrangement I made was ideal for me. I hired an independent financial advisor, but arranged to pay him for his advice only. He put together a long-term financial plan for me, tailored to my risk comfort level. Then I took his advice and did the investing myself. It was a lot of work, maybe too much for many people. However, I felt more in control, and more confident that he had no reason to recommend anything that wasn't ideal for me. Also, I learned a lot about investing, IRAs, taxes, the economy and the types of investments that are available.

My plan consisted of a combination of certificates of deposit (CDs) and mutual funds. I wanted nothing to do with individual stocks after I lost a lot of money as a result of a takeover battle my company went through, some poor real estate investments and other bad investments I had made during my working life. The mutual funds were a wide assortment covering many types of organizations. The CDs enabled me to live on that money for several years, so I could cash in the mutual funds when they are at my financial goal level, whenever that is. Also, CDs are predictable in that you know the interest rate from the beginning. Most advisors recommend "laddering" the CDs, that is, having CDs with varying maturity dates, so that they mature when you need the money. In general, you are penalized for cashing in a CD before the maturity date, so you must plan well.

**An investment portfolio is the set of all types of investments you have (stocks, bonds, mutual funds, property, financial instruments, etc.)

Note that CDs pay varying levels of interest, depending on the economy. Some CDs I bought around 2000 to 2002 paid as much as 7½% interest. However, during 2009 to 2012, interest rates were sometimes as low as 1%. Of course, interest rates on CDs have a relationship with inflation, so a low interest return on a CD corresponds with low inflation. However, the percentage return on investment on CDs and mutual funds determines how much money you will have to live on if this is your sole source of income.

The disadvantage of handling my own investments is that I don't always know the best, most efficient way to get the investments done. It often takes a lot of work to take money from one investment and move it into another one. Also, sometimes a financial person has found out I have control of my finances, and wants me to put some money into something they thought was a "no-lose" proposition.

However, if I had let my advisor handle my investments, I would have freed up a lot of my time and avoided discussions with acquaintances who wanted to advise me on how to invest part of my money. I could have just said, "All my money is tied up with my financial advisor. I can't even consider other possibilities."

Whichever way you decide to go, don't take a lump sum unless you are willing to believe you need some good quality financial help in investing it wisely and safely.

Financial Tips

When I set up my investment plan, my financial advisor gave me several good tips. Here are the best of them.

- Don't finance anything but your house. The interest rate on a loan is always higher than the interest rate on your savings. It is cheaper for you to withdraw money from your savings than to get a loan to finance anything.

- If you have enough money in your lump sum pension, savings, investments, etc., you probably don't need life insurance. If life insurance pays any interest at all, the rate will be lower than the rates you'll likely get from your investments. You may be better off cashing in your insurance and putting the money into your investment portfolio.

- Hire an attorney and set up a living trust, a will, a power of attorney, a health care representative, a living will, and related documents. These, along with an estate plan for your beneficiaries, will help your family avoid unnecessary taxes, fees and paperwork after you are gone.

How to Choose a Financial Advisor

Interview at least two or three financial advisors. Decide what service your want. Do you want someone who will handle your investments (you give them your money and they invest it for you), or someone who will give you advice and let you do the investing? That decision will help you decide which firm is the best type of advisor for you.

Here are some likely services that you might want from a financial advisor: Portfolio Management; Estate Planning; Insurance Advice; Retirement Planning; Asset Protection Strategies; and Tax Advice.

How does the person get paid? If the person will handle your investments, he or she will probably expect a percentage of your overall portfolio. If the person is giving you advice, he or she will charge you a fee based on the services provided and how long it takes the advisor to put together your plan.

Ask about the advisor's background. How long in business? What designation and/or license does the person or firm have? That is, does the person have a state license? What type of education does the person have?; e/g., Chartered Financial Consultant (ChFC), Certified Financial Planner (CFP), Certified Public Accountant (CPA), Chartered Life Underwriter (CLU), or attorney (JD).

Are you comfortable with the individual? If he or she talks fast and uses a lot of terms you don't understand, then he or she might not be right for you. You should feel that the person understands your level of knowledge and takes the time to make sure you understand what they are suggesting. He or she should try to determine how much risk you are comfortable instead of pushing high-risk or unusual investments on to you.

Remember, many supposedly smart athletes and celebrities have been cheated out of millions by fast-talking sham-artists who tell them they will make huge profits from their investments. An honest advisor will tell you that the safest investments pay small returns. Depending on the economy, conservative investments may pay as low as 2 to 4% return on your money per year. Around 1999, investments often paid 8-10%, but that was an unusual time. Make sure you understand the risks involved in the investments that are recommended to you. Since I retired, every change I have made in my investment portfolio has been to make it more conservative and reliable, even though the amounts I was earning became a little smaller.

The old saying, "there is no such thing as a free lunch," is especially true in investing for your retirement. The only investments that are truly safe are CDs and bank accounts that are protected by the Federal Deposit Insurance Corporation (FDIC).

Chapter Eight
Going Back to Work

After three and a half years of retirement, I went back to work. My investments had not worked out as well as expected. The economy was poor, and many of our retired friends were also having financial difficulties.

I didn't plan to go back to work, but it was a great opportunity near home, with reasonable hours, little responsibility and fair pay. I thought it would help my financial situation if I worked part-time for a few months. Unfortunately, it turned out to be a full-time, contracting job, although for just a few months.

Boy, if you ever start taking the joys of retirement for granted, just go back to work for a while. It's tough getting up at a set time in the morning after you get into the habit of sleeping late. It's tough going to work every day, too. And it's difficult to reorganize your time after having freedom for so long.

I was able to adjust after a few weeks, but it wasn't easy. I had gotten into the habit of taking a brief nap most afternoons after lunch. That, of course, had to stop. I had taken on some of the chores my wife did every day, since she still worked. I had to try to give some of the chores back to her; but she didn't want them back.

I found I was less efficient than I had been when I was a worker. I had to relearn all the techniques of time management I had forgotten. For two months, I spent every weekday evening and nearly every hour of most weekends catching up with the chores and projects at home that I was committed to doing.

Also, since retiring I had taken on several volunteer jobs—a newsletter that I edited, leadership in an alumni group, a committee in a professional organization, lunches with a retiree group—many of these jobs I had to curtail or postpone. I had started some occasional daytime activities with friends, daily responses to email, and spur-of-the-moment overnight trips. All this had to change, and change quickly. Suddenly people who were used to calling or email me frequently couldn't get in touch with me. I had to tell people to contact me less frequently.

I don't regret it. It was good to be reminded so vigorously what I was enjoying about retirement. I needed to experience work to remember why I had retired.

A surprising benefit of going back to work in a temporary job was the satisfaction I felt from doing a good job. While my job was in the field (technical writing) that I had worked my whole career in, the specific work was much different in subject. Where I had written about construction, now I had to write about computer software and programming. I began my new job knowing nothing about these subjects. I had to work with some computer software tools that I had never worked with before, and others I had little experience with. I was concerned about whether I could learn all this new stuff—or that my learning curve would be too slow to allow me to be an asset in my job.

Well, I wasn't a rocket scientist of learning, but I picked things up much more quickly than I thought I would. I was productive in a week, and comfortable with most aspects of the work in a month. Sure I applied myself, but I impressed myself too. I could still learn!!

I also had to deal with a less-reliable memory than I used to have. The solution to that problem was to write things down. I wrote down a list of the work assignments I was to do and the work I had completed. If I learned a new technique or process, I wrote down the details of that too. I wrote down times and places for meetings I was to attend, and the names of people in the meetings as I met them. I actually got a reputation for having a good memory, since my notes helped me remember things that some of my coworkers forgot.

Note that I was taking advantage of things I had learned over a lifetime of work. The wisdom of age, you might say. I even excelled in some ways. I was able to bring some skills from my previous work to my new job—people skills, organizational skills, analytical skills—that impressed my new boss. I think he expected me to be slow on the uptake and was pleasantly surprised.

Best of all, I was eventually able to go through the whole experience of retiring a second time. The best thing about retirement is that you suddenly have control of your time, you have the freedom to do what you please, and you have the satisfaction of knowing you earned it. The same goes for retiring a second time. Retired people might be happier if they go back to work for a few months every time they become a little bored.

Going back to work also can help with a serious retirement problem. People who are not busy or active tend to become bored and then depressed. This is especially common after the newness of retirement wears off. Chapter 2 discusses the problems of depression in more detail, but a short-term job can bring back the excitement of retirement and remind you of how much better off you are with free time that retirement brings.

The contract job was working for a medical facility run by a doctor in northwest Indiana. Much of my job had to do with finding out what was wrong with an off-the-shelf medical software program the clinic was using by interviewing the employees who worked on computers. Then I wrote up the information along with recommendations for how to create a tailor-made software system that would be more efficient and cost-effective. I received a useful education in how medical billing and insurance works.

I have had a variety of other part-time or short-term full-time jobs during my years of retirement. A number of jobs were from companies in the construction industry. Most of these resulted from contacts I had made during my working years, or my reputation as a technical writer. These led me to form a consulting company that provided a few tax breaks for me.

Also, I worked teaching some classes at a local campus of Purdue University, teaching technical and business writing skills to engineering students. The benefits of that job were that I learned to connect with younger generation people and got the satisfaction of knowing that I might be helping them to better careers with the skills they were learning from me.

Best of all, I needed the part-time income, but if I got tired of the work or frustrated with the conditions, I could quit without hurting my opportunities for future jobs.

Especially in the current economy, many retirees will be forced to consider going back to work, whether it be because of inflation, disappointing investments, errors in judgments about how much money you need to live on, changing situations, demands by children or other family members, or other unexpected situations. Even when there are few good-paying full-time jobs available, there are good-paying part-time jobs, or low-paying temporary jobs available to retired seniors.

Chapter Nine

How Does Retirement Affect Getting Along with Your Spouse?

A few years before I retired I was invited to a retirement seminar held by my employer for employees within a few years of retirement age. Spouses were invited too. The purpose of the seminar was to give future retirees information about financial planning for retirement and start us thinking about what we would do as retirees. It was a great exercise.

At one point they asked each future retiree what concerns or fears they had regarding retirement. Then they asked the spouses what their concerns and fears were. My wife responded, "24 hours."

"What does that mean," asked the moderator.

My wife then explained that for the past 20 years I was gone more than twelve hours a day commuting from our home in northwest Indiana to downtown Chicago. At least one week a month I traveled out of town for five or six days at a time. That meant that we spent only about one-fourth of our waking hours in an entire week together.

She said she wasn't sure that she looked forward to having me home 24 hours a day. I realized that she had a valid point. It's one thing to be around someone for a couple of hours a day during the week, but yet another to be together all the time.

Oftentimes, a marital relationship remains stable because both partners know what to expect from the other. When one or the other is gone on a regular basis, the other has planned activities that consider the other's absence. For example, the at-home spouse may wash clothes or clean up the home or go shopping at times when the other partner is away. Reading or watching TV are activities a spouse may take advantage of when the other partner is away.

Anything that upsets that balance or stability can be discomforting. For instance, if the husband bowls every Wednesday night, the wife may make a habit of calling her mother or going out with a couple of friends. When the husband stops the bowling habit, it disrupts the wife's schedule.

When one person works away from home and the other is home most of the time, the person who is home gets used to a schedule. The

64

stay-at-home spouse is not only comfortable with that but may also be happy with it.

Sometimes when I traveled on business, my wife considered it a mini vacation. She didn't have to worry about cooking, cleaning up or accommodating my activities. She also had a little extra free time.

You can imagine how disruptive it could be for her if, suddenly, I was home all the time.

Before I retired, we discussed how to keep from getting on each other's nerves. Since I planned to do some consulting as well as personal work on my computer when I retired, I suggested that, during certain agreed-upon hours, I would be working in my home office (a converted bedroom) with the door closed. Thus, she could consider me to be "away at work" during those hours.

Also, I took advantage of my leisure time to do some traveling with another retired friend. We visited Civil War battlefields and attended athletic events—both were activities that my wife wasn't especially interested in. Thus I was gone nearly as much as when I had been working.

Finally, we planned a few extra vacation trips during the months following my retirement. This helped us get used to spending more time together under enjoyable circumstances. Also, it helped me to get out of my work habits, such as getting up at 4:30 am to go to work or keeping an eye on my watch to make sure I didn't miss any meetings.

All these things helped her to ease into my retirement mode. In your case, a little creative thinking, or ideas from your spouse, will help you to make the adjustment from predictable working hours, to the unpredictable hours of a retiree.

A few questions to ask are as follows: Should we get up at the same time in the morning when only one of us works so that we can spend a little time together first thing? Should I set up an office space or a "man cave" so I am out of the way for part of the day? Would it be helpful for me to be out of the house at certain times each day? What life style changes would help in making the retirement adjustment for the spouse? Would it help for me to take over some tasks that my spouse currently does?

Chapter Ten

Retirement Tips

Humans are creatures of habit. Habits are desirable under certain circumstances and undesirable under others. For example, if you are an athlete, repeating the same moves makes them automatic to your muscles. Automatic moves allow you to think about strategy and the game without worrying about basic movements. This is also true with most types of work.

For example, typing on a keyboard or cell phone can become automatic and fast. Most other jobs become faster and more efficient through repetition.

However, bad habits often create problems. Even good habits, when the situation changes, can be undesirable. As a retiree, many things in your life are changing. You are likely to want to get up at a different time in the morning. You may stay up later at night. You may have less need to be aware of the time. The clothes you are used to wearing may be inappropriate. Your attitude toward others may need to become different when you become a retiree.

You will want to change some habits in your life when you retire. I went on a long out-of-town vacation right after I retired. That helped me to forget about the process of going to work. Also, I stopped wearing a watch for several weeks to break the habit of looking at my watch every few minutes. I had to make an effort to change my habits in many instances.

So, as a new retiree, you should teach yourself to be capable of changing your habits. Most people will agree that it is not good to "get set in your ways." It may take an effort to replace undesirable or unneeded habits with new, more appropriate ones. A lot of the excitement in life is based on doing new things or doing old things in new ways. As a new retiree, there are exciting new adventures to experience. Don't let old habits prevent you from trying new things.

Appearance and Habits—Don't get out of the habit of good personal hygiene. Get some new clothes. Get rid of most of your working attire. Give it to the Salvation Army, or AMVETS, or your church, or some other worthy organization. Make a conscious effort to do different things when you get up in the morning. Have breakfast with your spouse. Have breakfast out with a friend or friends. Go out for a jog or walk before breakfast. Do a couple of chores first thing. The point is, vary your activities from the beginning of your day until the end.

Look Around—Open up your mind to opportunities to do new and exciting things. If you read the newspaper, look for things of interest to you. There are organizations for retirees that have activities nearly every day. Look for activities that you couldn't do as a worker but have the time to do now. For instance, I saw an article about a motion movie that needed extras for scenes being made locally. I applied for it and got to be in a Hollywood movie. I saw an article about volunteers being needed to clean up a park; that was a fun and worthwhile activity. Keep a part of your mind open all day so that you don't miss out on activities that you might enjoy or feel good about trying.

Keep Fit—It is harder to be in good physical condition as we get older. However, it is not impossible. You just have to spend more time and effort to reach fitness goals that will let you be more active.

Don't Sit Around—One of the laws of physics is that "a body at rest tends to stay at rest, but a body in motion tends to stay in motion." The older you get, the easier it is to sit down and stay down, so it may take some effort to get moving. However, when you get moving it is easy to keep moving.

I have a lot of evening activities. Some are club meetings and some are athletic endeavors. After dinner, I sit for a few minutes, gathering my energy. My wife will often say, "Bill, you don't look like you want to go out."

And she's right. I could just sit there. However, once I get up and out, I get excited about whatever I am planning to do and have no trouble staying active.

Chapter Eleven

Handicapped Retirees

Everyone is different from everyone else. Some of us are full of energy and physically fit. We can do anything we set our minds to. Others, especially those whose jobs involved sitting at a desk or some other activity that involved little or not exercise, will find increased activity difficult.

However, the most difficult situation can be for a person who is handicapped. And if the handicap involves the feet or legs, the difficulty is even greater.

A physical fitness instructor once told me that the legs are the most important element of fitness. If your legs are strong and fit, your body will be strong and fit. But, if you have problems with your feet, knees or legs, you will be grounded.

However, that does not have to be entirely true. In this day and age, most public places are designed to have access for handicapped people. True, it is not easy for a person in a wheelchair or with a cane or walker to get around, but it is possible.

The handicapped retiree will have to make a greater effort than the rest of us in order to enjoy the adventures available to the retiree. However, it is just as important for those with physical limitations to be active.

Being active, both physically and mentally, is critically important to being a happy, fulfilled, self-confident and positive person. The lists in Chapters 12 and 13 include many low-impact and limited mobility activities that may be appropriate for people who cannot be as active as they would like to be.

Chapter Twelve

What Do You Want to Do with Your Retirement Time?

Most retirees find that they have a lot less free time than they expected to have. If you retire from a demanding or stressful job, you'll find that, after you retire, you will slow down and take a little more time with everything. However, you'll likely forget that everything takes more time when you plan your day. Thus, you'll soon discover that you never seem to accomplish as much as you think you will accomplish each day.

In this chapter we'll talk about activities specific to your interests that will satisfy your need to have a sense of purpose and value. You'll find that this is most critical to your happiness. For most people, activities that are fulfilling to them are important to having a feeling of self worth.

You may find that your new activities take as much of your time as your work in your former life did. I think you also will need to have some fun every day. So, you are going to need three lists (you may not need to really write these things down, but for some people, it helps).

The first list is things that give you a sense of purpose or value to yourself, your community, or to others. What these are depends on you. Also, the number of things that are on the list also depends on you. If you are certain about what activities are best for you, you may have only one or two things on your list. People with short lists usually have given a lot of thought and planning to retirement years before they were ready to retire.

Most of us will have five to ten things on our lists and will try each activity in turn until we find one or two that we really like to do. One of my friends had five things on his list. They included becoming a member of the Coast Guard Auxiliary and giving lectures at a nearby university. The activity in the Coast Guard Auxiliary happily combined boating and fishing with helping other boaters who were in trouble. The lectures permitted him to pass on knowledge he had gained during his career with the satisfaction that students were impressed with what he was teaching.

The second, and much longer, list is fun things that you always wanted to do but didn't have the time for, and unexpected things that just come up on short notice, but sound interesting or fun.

There is a third list or type of list. During my working years, my wife and I went on many vacations to many different places. After one especially enjoyable vacation to Maine, we discussed the fact that for us, Maine would be a place we would like to visit again on a regular basis. That discussion led us to make a list of places we had visited that we would like to visit again, and things we had done before that we would like to do again. This list permitted us to evaluate places we hadn't visited, but would like to visit, against places we had visited but definitely wanted to visit again.

The same is true with activities. Some activities are a disappointment or just not suited to you. Others are enjoyable or satisfying in some way, but you wouldn't do them a second time. Still others are perfect for you, meaning that you wouldn't mind doing them every day. That is what the third list will do for you.

Here are some examples of things I did in my first few of years of retirement:

Swimming—I got a season pass to the local water park. I like the water, and a season pass was an inexpensive way to go. The water park provided an opportunity to swim, go on water slides and other types of water rides, get some sun, and meet people. It became one of my favorite places.

Movie Theaters—I went to the movies and then out to eat in the middle of the week when all the working people are at home. You'd be surprised how few people are out at night during the week. Sometimes I went with my wife, but since she still was part of the working population, I often went with a retired friend. It was much less hassle than going on weekends.

Sporting Events—I went to sporting events, like professional or college baseball, basketball, or hockey games in the middle of the week when the working people are at home. Again, it's easier to get into sports events on weekdays or weekday evenings. I especially like baseball, men's college basketball and women's college and pro basketball. Note that women's sports are usually less crowded, less expensive to attend and are less difficult to get good seats for. A friend, who I went to many sports events with, suggested that we consider women's sports for those reasons. It turns out that, in many ways, women's sports are just as competitive and enjoyable as men's sports.

Sports Tournaments—During my working life it was difficult to go to out-of-town sports events like college football bowl games. They usually came up on short notice (a few weeks) and it was difficult to plan vacations around them; my work required much planning and I had to plan vacations months ahead of time. I am an alumni of Purdue University, a school not known for championship teams. When they had a series of good years and went to several bowl games, I went with them. Also, I became interested in men's and women's basketball tournaments. I learned that the person with the most flexible schedule has the greatest advantage in planning to go to these tournaments on short notice. Who has a more flexible schedule than a retiree? I had always wanted to go to the Rose Bowl and was able to go six months after I retired.

Cruise Ships—I occasionally went on cruises on relatively short notice. Certain kinds of cruises and other vacations offer huge discounts to those who can plan to go on a few days notice. Also, many of the cruises are orientated to older people, so many of the people you are likely to meet on a cruise will be retired and close to your age.

Seasonal Work—We all have heard about various part-time jobs for seniors: the greeter, the sales person, etc., but there are some unusual and very satisfying part-time jobs as well. A very unusual one for me was working as Santa Claus. I was not really looking for a part-time job, but this came "out of the blue." My son-in-law works as manager of a garden center and he wanted something that might draw additional customers and create some excitement for families. So we purchased a medium-quality Santa suit with all the accessories and created a little house for Santa at the garden center. What was especially challenging and fun was interacting with young children. As a grandparent, I had some experience with children. It was very satisfying to find that I could encourage the kids to sit on my lap for pictures with "Santa" without them becoming scared.

Exercise—As part of my effort to get in the best possible physical shape, I set up a program at a fitness center. The program is intended to keep me in the best possible shape so I can enjoy all the new activities I am now trying without hurting myself or wearing myself out. I try to walk or run and lift some weights twice a week. This is especially important since many of us get lazy when we retire and need strong motivation to work out and get exercise. A fitness center will help with this motivation and will help you track your progress. Some fitness centers also offer a fitness evaluation program that allows you to track your improvement; sometimes they are free, but more often there is a nominal charge for them. They are definitely worth the cost in helping you to determine whether or not you are making progress, and at what rate. If your improvement is not satisfactory, you may want to change your fitness program.

Sports for Charity—I participate in charitable walks, runs, and bicycle rides. These vary in distance, with some walks up to 10 miles, some runs up to 26 miles and some bike rides up to 100 miles or more. I have met many interesting people, and some have become my friends. Also, I have fun, help charitable or community causes, and keep in shape. Also, it's a great way to get fresh air. Most of these are listed in local newspapers, but active people you associate with will tell you about them. They all have websites, so, once you know the name of the event or the charity that sponsors it, you will be able to go online and find out more about it. A couple of examples I have experienced are walks raising money and awareness for breast cancer and other forms of cancer; Lori's Ride, a bicycle ride that benefits the Visiting Nurses Association; and the "Hilly 100," a two-day fitness ride up and down 100 miles of hills in southern Indiana over two days. The "Hilly 100" is especially enjoyable, since there are 5,000 to 7,000 participants of all ages, with meal stops at outdoor parks and meadows featuring hot meals, music, and social interaction.

Play Sports—I participate in many sports and sporting activities. I have read that each sport or physical activity improves different sets of muscle groups, so more activities are likely to positively affect more parts of the body. I snow ski, ice skate, cross-country ski, bowl, play golf, go white-water rafting, take hikes, play volleyball (including water volleyball), play basketball, play soft ball and ride a bicycle. There is no end of athletic activities to try. An unexpected benefit to playing these sports is that several of the neighborhood kids from the ages of six to sixteen have come over to learn basketball and soft ball from me. I suppose my white hair makes me a grandfather figure who they are willing to listen to.

Teaching Sports to Kids—I have never been a great athlete, but I have played many sports and know how to play most sports. During the summers, while babysitting for my two grandsons, I tried to teach them how to play basketball, baseball, softball and other sports. I suffered from the typical problem faced by grandparents: Kids don't really think you know anything worthwhile. However, on a couple of occasions, neighbor kids came over and wanted to play. I found that they were more receptive to learning the sports, because I was a stranger who seemed to know what he was talking about. Next thing I knew, my *own* grandkids realized that they could learn from me. The point is that you can share your knowledge about sports with children with positive results. However, sometimes you have to work at it until they develop confidence in your teaching skills. Stay with it!

Play Recreational Activities—Examples of low-impact recreational activities are miniature golf and go-cart racing. Another easy activity is visiting a local arboretum and walking pleasant trails. Again, there are smaller crowds during the week for all these activities. Also, I found these to be great to do with my wife.

Dancing and Dance Lessons—When I first got married, my wife-to-be talked me into taking disco dance lessons at a school. We learned a lot about this form of dancing. Best of all, when we went to weddings, reunions, etc., we danced well together, looked like we knew what we were doing, and looked good. It was great fun. We still remember some of the turns and moves. With the recent interest in TV shows like "Dancing with the Stars," there is a lot of interest in learning ballroom dancing. My wife again talked me into taking lessons. Trust me, it was hard work. However, we learned a number of ballroom dance steps; in just eight weeks, we learned the basics of fox trot, rumba, waltz, cha-cha, and swing—all useful at social events. An unexpected benefit was that it was great exercise. Also, we met a lot of interesting people at the lessons.

Write a Family History—As we get older, we often develop an interest in our family history—where we came from, who were our forbears, etc. As a senior, you are the most appropriate one to gather information about your family and record it for younger generations. You may have memories that you can set down, or be in contact with distant relatives you can get information from, or have the time to search the internet, or go to the local library, or contact other sources of information. Doing this may give you a lot of satisfaction, since you are doing an important service for your family. When I did this, I took advantage of my research to contact cousins and other relatives to get information about dates of birth and death, names and other information, and, at the same time, rekindle relationships.

Write Other Types of History—Depending on your experience and interests, you may wish to write a history of your community, your grade school, your high school, your college, your church, your club, etc. When we reach retirement age, we usually have a better appreciation of the importance of documenting histories of various groups. I helped write a successful history about the community and high school that I am from. It was a very satisfying project because we sold a few thousand copies of the book and many people complimented me on the work I did.

Museums and Art Galleries—I never had much chance to really enjoy museums and art galleries during my working life. Even when I did go, I didn't have enough time to see everything. Now I can take as much time as I wish. Each time I go, I spend the day in just one or two parts of the museum or art gallery, but go into more detail. Also, I have discovered that some of these places offer free admission on certain weekdays for seniors.

Ballet, Opera, Plays, Musicals, Concerts—If you have never been to any of these, now is your chance. Be aware, however, that sometimes these events require getting used to. They are an acquired taste. If you learn how to appreciate them, they can be really entertaining. It's a great chance to try something new.

Local Travel—For many seniors, travel, even local travel, can be difficult. Driving a car in the city can be dangerous for those of us who are older and have slower reflexes. At the very least, driving around town can be less than enjoyable. If you are fortunate to live in an area with good public transportation, you can get around more easily. I often go into the city on a commuter train with friends. We have fun talking on the train, and avoid the hassle of driving. Also, it is surprisingly cheap. I can ride the train into Chicago round trip for $7.00. This train, along with subways and buses in Chicago, offers substantial discounts to seniors.

Air Shows, Community Events—I've been able to attend and enjoy air shows, taste events, jazz fests, and many other seasonal activities in my area. Again, the crowds are smaller during the week, especially during traditional working hours. Avoid the crowds; you'll enjoy the events more when attendance is sparse.

Become an "Extra" in a Hollywood Movie—In the northwest Indiana/Chicago area, there are various kinds of Hollywood or made-for-TV movies being made all the time. Frequently the movie producers are looking for "extras," that is, inexperienced actors to be in the background of scenes. A Tom Hanks movie, "Road to Perdition," was being made in the Chicago area a few years ago and I was hired as an extra. I was in four scenes, including two with Tom Hanks. It was a truly unique and educational experience. I had my hair and mustache cut for the era of the movie, wore a costume and carried props for my roles. Again, it was very educational, fun and unusual (and I even got paid and fed). Most often, searches for extras are mentioned in the local newspapers. Watch for them. Naturally, most filming is done during the week—an advantage for retirees.

Combine Social and Physical Fitness Activities—Sometimes it is hard to motivate myself to get the exercise I need. For me, doing some type of exercise with other people makes it easier to do what I *should* do.

The ski club I belong to has a group of members that go out biking, roller blading, and/or hiking every Tuesday night at a trail that once was railroad tracks. We do 10-20 miles, talk to each other as we ride, blade, or hike, then go out for pizza and drinks afterward. The club also has other physical activities to help keep us in shape for winter skiing, including canoeing, playing volleyball, and throwing a football around. Making what is good for you into a fun activity makes it easier to do.

Walking Groups or Clubs—As I mentioned above, exercising with others is more motivating. In the town I live in, Valparaiso, IN, fitness is surprisingly popular. There are competitive runs and walks, bike rides, snowshoeing, cross-country skiing, and other sports to keep people fit. The Parks Department even has an activity called "Fit City," which sponsors activities for anyone interested. Among other things, I participate in a walk at 5:30 pm one afternoon a week. There may be a few or many people show up. Most are adults and some are seniors. The group is led by a fitness person who helps make it fun and worthwhile physically.

Participate in Senior Games (Sometimes Called Community Games)— Early in my retirement I discovered local "Community Games," where I could compete with others in my age group for medals that look a little like Olympic medals. They involve a wide variety of sports and activities (as diverse as 100-meter dash, miniature golf, bowling, dancing, Pinochle, swimming, walking, Bocce Ball, etc.). These are also held at the state and national level. They are mainly intended for people of retirement age, but they are often open to those as young as 50 years. I did very well in these games, but more importantly, they forced me to target certain muscle groups to prepare for specific sporting competitions.

Become an Adjunct Professor—Quite by accident I was invited to teach at the college level. As a technical writer with 40 years of experience, I found that my services could be helpful to engineering students. I didn't think I would be good at it, but I found that my knowledge and experience provided these young people with a way to help them make their careers more successful. Best of all, I make a little part-time income teaching technical and business writing and technical report writing while enjoying the respectability of teaching at the college level. One of the best benefits for me was finding out that there was less of a generation gap with the students than I expected. As a result of this activity, I am now much more comfortable with younger family members, such as nephews and nieces, than I had been before.

Pledge Drives—Another activity that came up by accident was participating in PBS (public TV) pledge drives. We have two local PBS (Public Broadcasting System) stations and each has periodic pledge drives. In both cases, the stations invite local organizations to come in and answer the phones in the evenings during the pledge drives (to earn money to run the station). Two different organizations I am affiliated with were invited to participate in it. It was lots of fun. We had tours of the TV station, were fed, were treated well, and were trained on what to do. The benefits for us were that we were helping a worthy cause and our friends and families got to see us on TV.

Radio Announcer—I know this sounds a little "off the wall," but it really is a possibility. I had been a radio "disc jockey" in college with some success. As a retiree I thought about whether I could be successful working on a local radio station during the hours that seniors are listening. I thought I could be a real success. One day a local station posted an ad looking for local people to do shows. The station suggested that no experience was necessary, so I applied. It turned out they were not hiring, but were looking for contributors. If I could have attracted sponsors to pay for my time, I could have had a show. Anyway, while that didn't work out as I expected, it really was a lot of fun. I created a one-hour show with music, interviews, discussions of subjects of interest to seniors, and a little humor. It was a fun and educational experience creating a show and seeing what goes on behind the scenes in radio.

TV Announcer—A related experience was a group tour, sponsored by a local seniors group, to visit a TV studio in Chicago. As part of the tour, volunteers read the news off of teleprompters (the things newscasters use to read material without having to look down). We all learned a lot about how newscasts were done, and those of us who tried to read the news in front of a TV camera received a video of the "newscast" to take home.

Barefoot Cruise—Unusual vacations give you an opportunity to experience the "road not taken." My wife and I went on a Windjammer barefoot cruise on a sailing ship and found an adventure that was most enjoyable and unexpected. Among other things, it was the most "adult" vacation we had ever been on. It was amazing how different an experience can be when it is "adults only." Island tours, as well as activities on the ship, were especially orientated to adults. This wasn't a "senior" group, although maybe one-fourth of the participants were over 50. But there were jokes, games, drinking and other activities that were more "adult" than I had experienced. You could even be a volunteer crew member and "hoist the sails." It was a kind of fun that many people would really enjoy. A company with a similar type of cruise is Island Windjammers (www.islandwindjammers.com).

Jury Duty—Seniors make really good jurors because of our life experiences. I don't know if you can volunteer for jury duty, but it certainly is a satisfying way to spend some time. I was called up for jury duty and the process taught me a lot about our court system, both good and bad. However it was a great learning experience, and I got paid for it. Best of all, I learned that jury duty is one of our most important obligations or privileges of citizenship, besides serving in the military. I felt very good about my efforts on the jury. Younger people often make the mistake of trying to avoid jury duty, but I think it gives a person an important education about how our judicial system works, and why it is so highly respected by people in other countries.

Historical Monuments—Many retirees are interested in history. If you have the time and like to travel, a great past-time is visiting historical monuments, parks and sites. For example, in the first month after I retired, my wife and I flew to Boston to enjoy some sea food. While we were there, we learned that there are many famous historical sites. The variety is wide. We had a drink at the bar that was used for the TV sitcom, "Cheers." We visited a couple of Revolutionary War sites, such as the site of the Boston Massacre. Then we discovered the Freedom Trail, which takes about three hours and covers 16 of the most important Revolutionary War sites. It was amazing (http://www.cityofboston.gov/freedomtrail/). Another thing I had always wanted to do was to visit some of the most significant Civil War battle fields. A retired friend and I have visited something like 20 major battle fields, such as Gettysburg and Antietem, over the past ten years. There are hundreds of historical places to visit in the U.S. Most are well preserved and include guides, museums, places to eat and gift shops.

Class Reunions—As people near the end of their working lives, they often develop a new or renewed interest in class reunions and/or their cultural roots. The reason for that is simple. As we work and raise a family, we focus on the future: promotions, raises, our next job, affording family needs, etc. Time is spent working or dealing with family obligations. We often have little time to remember the friends and classmates we had when we were growing up. However, as our focus switches to the past, we begin to appreciate our roots.

Often our 40th, 45th and 50th reunions hold more interest for us and, as a result, are better attended and more fun. As we get older and more mature, we may find that we have more appreciation for our classmates and friends from high school or college days. I found that some of the petty differences, cliques, educational differences, and other things that might have kept us apart while in school no longer matter.

Reunion Committees—Besides attending high school and/or college reunions, you may find working on a reunion committee to be fulfilling and fun. For the first few reunions we had, I did not serve on the reunion committee. However, circumstances made me manager of my high school 44-year class reunion. I had a great time, and as a result of having never served on the committee before, I found myself generating new ideas that made the reunion more fun and different from the previous reunions. You'll have fun working with old friends you may not have seen in years. Also, you will find that you are able to make a big contribution to the enjoyment of your classmates.

Revisiting Your Cultural Roots—Like our school experiences and class reunions, maturity often brings a new appreciation for our cultural roots. A person may be too busy with his or her career and personal life to think much about his or her national origin, race or culture. Also, these things often take a back seat when we are trying to minimize the importance of race, culture or religion in the workplace. But with age and a change in our working status, these things can become more important to us. As we enter our "golden years," maturity and life-learning show us that our cultural roots can give us a greater perception of where we came from and why we are the way we are. It is important to take pride in national origin, race, religion, where our families came from, our cultural traditions, etc.

A friend of mine who had served in the military and the government never had much time for considering his cultural roots during his working years. However, when his mother passed away, he became involved in the religious traditions of his family and cultural background. He became reacquainted with members of his parents' church and their traditions, including music. Also, because he was nearing retirement, he developed a new appreciation for these things. Although he lives in Florida, he now returns to northwest Indiana every year to attend and participate in SerbFest, a Serbian Orthodox Cultural Festival. He even volunteers (along with other members of his family) to help make the festival a success. He has a great time with old family friends and new friends who share his Serbian culture.

These cultural festivals can be fun too, even if you do not share the particular culture. A local Polish festival, called Pierogi Fest, pokes fun at Polish traditions and entertains all. Whether you are Polish or not, you'll have a good time, and you'll be able to sample the Polish cuisine. Authentic cultural dances, events and foods blend with a "beauty queen," Miss Paczki, and other humorous kinds of entertainment. Other local festivals that are fun for many of us are celebrations of the traditions of Greek, Italian, German, Swedish, Irish and Scottish cultures, to name a few. Different parts of the country have different festivals and traditions. Some of these events are fun, but all are educational and interesting. Most also provide the opportunity to sample ethnic foods at their best.

There are many other types of festivals and events to visit, besides the cultural ones, especially in summer. Jazzfest (music), Air & Water Show, Taste of (insert any name) are some Chicago-area events I've enjoyed. I recall a cherry festival in southern Indiana, a lobster festival in Maine and a peanut festival in Georgia, for instance.

Chapter Thirteen

Things to Do and Places to Go

The examples of activities described in Chapter 12 are just a few of the things I have tried since I retired. All are satisfying, fulfilling, exciting or fun. Some are good for fitness; others are good for mental exercise.

For the list below, I wanted to suggest at least *One Hundred Things You Can Do.* This way you will have some real variety in activities to try. This list is a compilation of those activities I experienced myself, those my friends told me about, and those I have heard about from acquaintances. Some require a high level of fitness while others are suitable for those with physical limitations. I have tried to indicate those that are especially appropriate for those with physical limitations, or those with other special needs, such as for singles. Note that some activities are listed on both lists when they are appropriate for both active and limited-mobility people.

Low-Impact Activities. Many seniors have handicaps that prevent them from participating in sports and fitness activities. Several of the following activities can appeal both to those who are active and fit as well as those with handicaps that limit their activity.

1. Low-impact outdoor games—Everyone needs to spend time outside, as sunshine is important to good health. Unfortunately, many sports and activities are difficult for those who are handicapped or have limited mobility. However, many communities have games that nearly anyone is able to play. For example, bean bag and horseshoes can be played standing or sitting, and only require strength in the arms. Bocce Ball involves throwing one ball to try to hit or be close to another ball. There are many more outdoor games that can be considered.

2. Card games—Every senior center I know of offers card games on a weekly basis or open activities that can include card games every day. Some card games, such as pinochle and

bridge, have their own organizations for those who are experienced card players. Often you can find people who are less expert, but interested, in playing such games as euchre, poker, blackjack, and old maid, as well as pinochle and bridge.

3. Reading cartoons—After I retired, I found that reading the morning newspaper was a novelty. I had never had much time to spend with the paper on work days, so taking my time with it was really enjoyable. Besides news and sports, I enjoyed doing some of the games (Sudoku, crossword, etc.); and I found the cartoons gave me a laugh every morning. Over time, I realized that cartoons also provide a contemporary view of the changes in society. That is, I was learning how people's views change, and how today's problems are dealt with by modern families. When you think about it, those cartoons provide more than just humor; they provide an education about the changes in the world that most retirees may not have easy access to. Of course, reading the newspapers also keeps you up-to-date on local, national and international news and events.

4. Board games—Your local senior center is likely to help you find players for board games, such as Monopoly, if that is your preference. You'll also make friends, but if you are homebound, I know for a fact that you can buy electronic Monopoly and find players from the comfort of your own home via the internet. This applies to some other board games too. Using the internet, you can schedule and play games online.

5. Join a band or orchestra if you like music and can sing or play—One of my friends joined a band in San Antonio; it plays concerts and dances and marches in parades. My

father-in-law joined a similar band in Indiana, called the Rusty Pipes. In both cases, music provided discipline and satisfaction—the discipline to practice regularly and the satisfaction of entertaining large groups of people. This is also an opportunity to make friends. This can be low-impact or highly physical depending on whether you join an organization that simply plays or one that marches and plays. Practicing and playing music is also good exercise for the mind.

6. Get a pet—Pets provide great companionship and are often emotionally helpful to people who are not very mobile. Pets, especially dogs, provide companionship and love. However, if you have never had a pet before, know that pets require attention and care from you. They cannot be left alone for long. However, if you will be traveling, you can always put up your pet in a kennel; many provide a resort-style environment for pets.

7. Share your expertise or experience—If you belong to a professional organization, a trade union, or some other organization having to do with your business, trade or profession, you may have experience or expertise that can be helpful to younger workers. Contact the appropriate organization and find out if they would be interested in having you speak, or meet with members of your business, trade or profession. It can be fulfilling and enjoyable for you, but it can be career changing for the younger people who you interact with.

8. Write a book—Many organizations need people to help write books, brochures or articles about their history or their purpose. If you feel you have writing skills, you might volunteer your time to help write something. There is a lot of

satisfaction to helping out in this way, and the result is a tangible item that you can point to with pride.

9. Write a family history—As we get older, we often develop an interest in our family's history—where we came from, who our forbears were, etc. As a senior, you are the most appropriate one to gather information about your family and record it for younger generations. Doing this may give you a lot of satisfaction, since you are doing a big service for your family.

10. Write other types of history—Depending on your experience and interests, you may wish to write a history of your community, your grade school, your high school, your college, your church, your club, etc. When we reach retirement age, we usually have a better appreciation of the importance of documenting histories of various groups and organizations. One acquaintance of mine was hired by his company to write a corporate history after he retired.

11. Write a newsletter—Practically every organization has some type of newsletter, whether it be on paper, via email, or on a website. If you have minimal writing and editing skills, you may find this activity especially satisfying and appreciated. I wrote and edited a newsletter for a ski club I belonged to. It was fun and useful, the members appreciated my efforts, and the local ski council gave me an award for my efforts.

12. Go to the movies—It's very relaxing to go to the movies or out to eat alone or with friends in the middle of the week when all the working people are at home. You'd be surprised how few people are out at night during the week.

13. Go out to breakfast—One of my neighbors goes out with several friends to a carryout coffee place nearly every morning. It's not fancy, but it is inexpensive and the place doesn't seem to mind how long his group stays. Of course, you can do this with your spouse or a good friend, too. I go out with a friend or my wife an average of once a week. It is a relaxing way to start the day.

14. Sports events—Going to sporting events, like baseball, basketball, or hockey games, in the middle of the week when the working people are at home, can be fun and inexpensive. Again, it's easier to get into sports events on weekdays or weekday evenings. Often there are local schools or community sports that are as entertaining as the big time.

15. Easy and economical sports events—In the Chicago area, professional sporting events are often expensive and tickets are hard to get. Also, a nearby university has a team I like to follow and

is likewise inaccessible to me. However, a friend of mine and I realized that women's sporting events can be just as entertaining as the men, but cost much less and have better ticket availability. We now go to a lot of women's basketball games at both the college level and the pros. We get great seats and good prices, and can decide to go on the spur of the moment if we wish.

16. Sports tournaments—Going to college football bowl games and basketball tournaments on short notice can be lots of fun; these are usually planned on only two to four weeks notice and the person with the most flexible schedule has the advantage in planning to go. Who has a more flexible schedule than a retiree?

17. Cruise ships—Retirees can go on cruises on short notice. Certain kinds of vacations offer huge discounts to those who can plan to go on a few days notice. Cruise ships are great places to meet people in your age group, although they may not live near you.

18. Museums, art galleries, zoos—Many of these places have the facilities to help those with handicaps or that have physical limitations. As a retiree you can now take as much time as you wish to learn and enjoy. Many museums and art galleries offer free admission on certain weekdays or other occasions. However, watch out for days of school visits. A thousand screaming children can limit your enjoyment of exhibits.

19. Air shows, taste events, community activities—Most of these kinds of events are handicap-friendly. However, there is often a lot of walking involved, so you may need to provide for your physical limitations. Bigger communities and cities have air shows, taste events, jazz fests, or other seasonal activities. Chicago has something just about every week during the summer. Even smaller communities have some type of annual event. Again, the crowds are smaller and more senior-friendly during the week.

20. Unusual museums—Some communities have very unusual museums that can provide specialized knowledge and experience. A local broadcast museum taught me about the history of radio and TV broadcasting, including being able to hear and see programs from the past (my past as a child). I also was given the opportunity to read the news from a teleprompter and get a tape of my experience as an "anchor man." There are museums featuring different ethnicities, events, types of art, sports, war, etc.; for example, three unusual museums in Chicago deal with Polish ethnic information, the Holocaust and Lake Michigan ships.

21. Further your education—Most of us have some subject we want to learn more about. Local colleges and universities often offer classes to the general public, and communities usually offer adult-education classes. Learn about such diverse subjects as history, a second or third language, crafts,

computers, family law, email, finance, retirement investing, etc. The list is endless, and your benefits are learning and challenging your mind (which can help prevent mental deterioration, such as dementia).

22. A puzzling activity—For those who can't handle a lot of physical activity but want to tax their brains, I think old-fashioned jigsaw puzzles are a great repast. They force you to visualize how a certain shape will fit with other pieces. Doing puzzles is also a very relaxing and entertaining activity. There are many other types of puzzles that exercise the brain: crosswords, ciphers, Sudoku, word sleuths, etc. I have grown to especially like Sudoku. Computer games of various sorts range from complex high-powered games to simple solitaire.

23. Email—Many retirees have had little experience with computers and find them hard to understand. However, a computer is a terrific tool for retirees—especially those with physical limitations. Email permits you to communicate with friends and acquaintances all over the world, and do it from home

or at a time and place of your choosing. You email someone when it is convenient to you, and they reply when they have the time to do it. Most communities have classes in learning to operate a computer and how to understand email.

24. Historical monuments—Many retirees are interested in history. If you have the time and like to travel, a great pastime is visiting historical monuments, parks and sites. Of course, Washington, D.C., has many historical places and museums, but there are important historical places all over the United States. For example, there are state and national Civil War battlefield sites in something like 20 different states. The East Coast is loaded with Revolutionary War historic places, such as the Freedom Walk in Boston and the Battle of Yorktown in Virginia, where the Revolutionary War was won. Some of these sites involve a lot of walking, but most can accommodate people with disabilities.

25. Class reunions—As people near the end of their working lives, they often develop a new or renewed interest in reunions of grade or middle schools, high schools or colleges. The reason for that is simple. As we work and raise a family, we focus on the future: promotions, raises, our next job, affording family needs, etc. Time is spent working or dealing with family obligations. We often have little time to remember the friends and classmates we had when we were growing up. However, as our focus switches to the past, we begin to appreciate our roots. Often our 40th, 45th and 50th reunions hold more interest for us and, as a result, are better attended and more fun. As we get older and more mature, we may find that we have more appreciation for our classmates and friends from our high school or college days. And usually the petty differences, cliques, educational differences and other things that

might have kept us apart while in school no longer matter. A very satisfying and enjoyable activity is to either serve on or manage a class reunion committee for your high school or other educational institution. You'll have fun working with old friends you may not have seen in years. Also, you will find that you are able to make a big contribution to the enjoyment of your classmates.

26. Revisiting your cultural roots—Like our school experiences and class reunions, maturity often brings a new appreciation for our cultural roots. A person may be too busy with his or her career and personal life to think much about his or her national origin, religion, race or culture. Also, these things often take a back seat when we are trying to minimize the importance of race, culture or religion in the workplace. But with age and a change in our working status, these things can become more important to us. As we enter our "golden years," maturity and life-learning show us that our cultural roots can give us a greater perception of where we came from and why we are the way we are. It is important to take pride in national origin, race, religion, where our families came from, our cultural traditions, etc. Activities in learning more about or revisiting your cultural roots can include research on your computer, visiting libraries and museums, attending culture-based festivals, seeking out people to network with, and taking classes.

Higher Levels of Fitness. The activities listed above are not just for people with limited mobility or health problems. They can be extremely interesting, enlightening and satisfying for all retirees. However, for those who are physically active or want to improve their fitness level, or just want a higher level of physical activity, the following activities will help you achieve a desired fitness level, as well as keep you busy.

27. Swimming—Get a season pass to the local water park, pool, or some other type of park that you enjoy. Even if you are not able to swim, it is really enjoyable to get out in the fresh air and sunshine, and a season pass is an inexpensive way to go. Another alternative is a fitness center, like YMCA, that has a pool.

28. Fitness—If you plan to be active, or if you had a job in which you sat most of the day, or if you want to exercise to reduce your weight, you should try to find the appropriate exercise program that will prepare you to do the activities you want to do. Most fitness centers will help you set up a program that helps you achieve the highest level of fitness considering your physical or health limitations. For instance, some exercises, like aquacise, are helpful for people with arthritis. Depending on your needs and expectations, there are many types of fitness centers—at a wide range of costs. However, to avoid injury it is important to find a fitness center that has experts who can help you design a program that fits your needs and desires without pushing you to the point of injury. Examples of goals you might have are: strength-training, weight-control, stamina, preparation for specific activities or sports, etc. For the person nearing retirement, you may want to prepare in advance for increased physical activity. Another benefit of a fitness center is that some of them offer a fitness evaluation program to help you track your fitness improvement.

29. Setting fitness goals—Whatever your level of fitness, you should set fitness goals to achieve the level of fitness you desire. Most fitness centers will help you set up a program that keeps you fit enough to enjoy all the new activities you are now trying. Also, fitness professionals will work with you to create the program that will help you achieve whatever goals you have. For instance, one set of exercises will help you lose

weight; another will sculpt your body; still another will prepare you for a specific activity, such as skiing, running, etc.

30. YMCA or other fitness center tournaments—Many fitness centers have athletic competitions to make exercise fun. These are
usually easy for people of any age, but some are tougher than
others. I have participated in "Walking Across America," where
you try to walk hundreds of miles during a certain period of days
or months, "The Million Step Club," where you walk one million
steps in 20 weeks, and the mini Triathlon, where you swim for
a certain number of minutes, then ride a bicycle machine for a
certain number of minutes, then walk or run on a treadmill for a
certain number of minutes. In most cases, if you complete the program in the required days or time, you get a T-shirt or some other
item of clothing or award with the name of the competition on it.

31. Charitable events—You may wish to participate in charitable
walks, runs, or bike rides. These vary from a few miles to ten
miles for walks, three to 26 miles for runs, and 15 to 100
miles or more for bike rides. You'll meet some interesting
people, have fun, help charitable or community causes, and
keep in shape. Also, it's a great way to get some fresh air in
the spring, summer and fall.

32. Play sports—There are many sports and activities you can participate in, depending on your physical condition and skills.
You can downhill ski, snowboard, ice skate, cross-country ski,
bowl, play golf, play basketball, swim, play volleyball (including less-demanding water volleyball), ride a bike, go canoeing
or rowing, throw around a softball or football, play bean bag
toss, run, walk, speed walk, roller skate or roller blade, fish,
hunt, etc. There is no end of athletic activities for you.

33. Recreational activities—This is another limitless group of activities. Miniature golf is great for seniors. Again, there are
smaller crowds during the week. I found this to be a great

activity to do with one's spouse, as long as he or she (or perhaps you) are a good loser.

34. Movie or TV extra—Depending on where you live, there may be an occasional opportunity to play an extra in a Hollywood movie or made-for-TV movie. It's fun, interesting and you may meet a star. One of my friends was in one of the "Gambler" series of TV movies, and was "promoted" to a speaking part. As a result, he was able to hang out with the stars of the movie. Most often, searches for extras are mentioned in the local newspapers. Watch for them.

35. Combine sports with social activities—Many clubs and community organizations have events that permit you to combine social and physical fitness activities, like bike rides, walks, volleyball games, etc. It's great to go out for a couple of hours of good physical activity, then head to a restaurant for beverages (adult or otherwise), pizza or other food, and social interaction.

36.   Bicycle riding—This is one of the best outdoor physical activities because it fits people at a variety of physical levels, but provides great scenery and fresh air too. Even on a hot day, the speed you ride will keep you cool. In most areas there are railroad right-of-ways that have been converted to bike trails. The bike trails are usually scenic, often go through or near desirable destinations, offer an opportunity to meet other bike riders, and are a great group activity. There are many organizations that have rides that allow you to ride with others of your age or physical fitness level. There are bicycle riding clubs, bike shops that organize rides, charitable organizations with rides, etc. The ski club I belong to has bike rides every week from May to November to help skiers keep in shape during the off season.

37.   Cycling adventures—For those who want to take bike riding to a higher level, there are organizations that arrange multi-day bike riding adventures that include meals and accommodations,

and often include a bike for you to ride. Indiana has one of the most popular and difficult rides anywhere, the Hilly Hundred. It consists of 50 miles a day of various-difficulty hills around the Bloomington, Indiana, area for two days. Several thousand riders from the ages of pre-teens to 80s ride together; there are three meal stops a day with live music, hot food, and friendly people.

38. Bowling—This is a slightly lower-impact type of sport. You can choose to go by yourself or with a friend, or you may join a bowling league. It's fun, competitive and social. Many of the people in today's bowling leagues are over 70, so it is definitely a sport for all ages. Also, there are leagues for men, women, seniors and mixed groups.

39. Go-cart racing—You've got to be physically flexible to do this, but go-cart racing is certainly exciting and fun. It's a riot to go racing with several friends.

40. Dancing—There are numerous organizations that have dances. For example, there are some communities that have

clubs devoted strictly to square dancing. Don't laugh, they tell me they have a lot of fun and good social interaction. Many organizations that have dances for seniors offer the opportunity for singles to meet with and dance with partners they meet at the dance.

41.   Dance lessons—With the recent interest in TV shows like "Dancing with the Stars," there is a lot of interest in learning ballroom dancing. It seems like there are 20 to 30 organizations in my area offering ballroom dance lessons. To my surprise, it turns out that learning to dance is great exercise. Even better, learning dance steps makes your mind more active and helps prevent dementia. Furthermore, dancing can burn 370 calories per hour (for someone weighing 150 pounds) and even prevents or slows loss of bone mass. I learned the basics of fox trot, rumba, waltz, cha-cha, and swing in just eight weeks. Also, there are social groups formed from these dance lessons; groups for square dancing, ballroom dancing, salsa dancing, etc., get together every week or two. It's a great way to meet members of the opposite sex.

42.   Square dancing—Many areas have square dancing clubs. They are lots of fun, provide good exercise, and are a source for making friends.

43.   Walking—This simple activity can lead to lots of enjoyment and a higher level of fitness than you might imagine. Since walking is easy on the knees, it is less likely to cause injury than some other more-vigorous forms of exercise. You can walk by yourself, or with a friend or spouse; you can walk slow or fast; you can walk short or long distances; you can walk in scenic areas or in urban areas; you can combine walking with charitable events, such as the March of Dimes Walk or the Three-Day Walk for Breast Cancer; and you can walk indoors

or outdoors. Extremely hot climates and wintry-weather climates usually have "Mall Walking" or walking in schools, gymnasiums or social centers where you can walk indoors when necessary.

44. "Fit City" walking—Many towns and cities have organized forms of exercise such as weekly walks. They are usually designed for people who are looking to improve their level of fitness, such as seniors. Check it out by calling your local park service or check your community's website.

45. Guided hikes—For those who get really serious about walking or hiking, you may want to look into the many organizations that offer vacations that include guided hikes or walks. These are available all over the world, and usually include meals and lodging arrangements. One company that offers guided package walks that I know of but have not yet tried is Classic Journeys (www.classicjourneys.com).

46. National Park tours—One of my friends told me about multi-day group hikes in National Parks. Specifically, Yosemite National Park in California has tours that are so popular that you have to sign up a year in advance. The program is to hike for several hours each day, then stay overnight at one of the Park's great lodges. Next morning you set out for another lodge. The Park moves your luggage for you. I heard it is a wonderful experience. It is likely that other national or state parks have similar packages.

47. Guided bicycle rides—There are also organizations that provide single-day or multi-day bike rides, including tour guides, meals and lodging. Although there are many companies that provide these tours, the following are a couple of websites to check (www.summerfeet.net; www.bicycletour.com; www.centralcoastoutdoors.com).

48. Adventure packages—There are many other kinds of guided tours or arranged combination packages. I went on a Western Adventure that included white-water rafting one day, an exciting Hummer 4x4 Safari the next day and a technical hike through part of Arches National Park the third day; the package included other options, such as staying at a luxurious ranch and horseback riding. This was through Western River Expeditions (www.westernriver.com). Note that some aspects of these adventures require a fairly high level of fitness.

49. Community or "Senior Games"—Whether they are called Senior Games, Community Games or something else, these are held at the local, state, and national level. They are mainly intended for people of retirement age, but usually are open to those as young as 50 years. They involve a wide variety of

sports and activities (as diverse as 100-meter dash, minia-ture golf, bowling, swimming, dancing, and Pinochle). Often they have 50 or more events over a two-week period, a little like the Olympics. You compete against people of your sex and age group (usually in five-year increments, such as men, 60-64). What an opportunity to meet and compete with peo-ple of your age and make use of whatever athletic skills you are able to maintain! My favorite aspect of Senior Games was that each year I targeted certain events I liked and set goals for getting physically fit to compete in them. It made getting into shape more fun.

50. Participate in winter sports—To maintain some level of fitness, it is usually necessary to exercise all year round. Many people find it difficult to achieve the level of motivation needed to work out at a fitness facility. Cross-country skiing, downhill skiing, downhill ski racing, ice skating, and snowshoeing are sports that you can participate in during winter, when other

activities may not be available. These sports provide a great way to get outside. Most of these sports allow you to choose an appropriate degree of difficulty depending on your health and fitness level. They are all more fun than working out on weight or fitness machines. However, note that downhill skiing requires a lot of leg muscle development, and can be dangerous if you're not in the proper shape. Still, I have friends who started skiing at an advanced age and did just fine. A good friend of mine began skiing at age 58 and by age 70 was ski racing on giant slaloms. One additional benefit of outdoor sports in winter is that being outdoors provides Vitamin D, which you need all year round.

51. Water volleyball—Some senior centers and fitness centers offer sports that are especially intended for seniors. A favorite for many seniors is water volleyball. It's low impact, like water walking, but works your legs and arms, and it is lots of fun because it is competitive. For older people with tight muscles, an hour or two of water volleyball really loosens you up; it really feels good. I believe water volleyball is also recommended for people with arthritis. In any event, people from as young as their 50s to as old as their 90s play this sport. For those people looking for something easier or something that will help with arthritis, many centers offer aquacise water exercises.

52. Buy a boat—If you live near a large body of water and like fishing or boating, you might want to buy a boat. Besides using it for recreation, you can do more with it. A friend of mine bought a small boat after he retired from a military career followed by several years with an important job as a civilian worker in the Defense Department. While he enjoyed fishing and the other joys of boating, he needed more fulfillment.

Ultimately, he joined the Auxiliary Coast Guard, and often served in support of the Coast Guard during busy holidays or in emergencies in the Tampa Bay area. His volunteer work benefits from his military experience, and he was "happy as a clam." You can also rent boats if your budget doesn't allow a purchase.

53. Get a computer—Many retirees don't realize what a resource a computer is. It provides entertainment; it is a resource for information; it makes shopping from home a breeze; but most of all it provides an easy means of communication. A good friend I worked with for many years has had both knees replaced and has a hard time getting out and about. He is able to maintain ties with friends and family through email. Also, the internet is an excellent resource for almost any kind of information, and it allows you to shop "till you drop" without ever leaving home.

54. Become a reinactor—One of my friends participates in historical performances as a reinactor. He says it is fun to dress up in costume and demonstrate how people lived in past generations. There are reinactors for the War Between the States, World War I and II, pioneer times, etc. Check around. We have a local baseball team, called the Deep River Grinders that plays baseball according to the gentlemanly rules of 1858. What a treat for the fans to be transported back to a more leisurely time. There are even rules of politeness for fans. A retiree must be able to run to play.

55. Volunteer professional skills for fun and profit—A steelworker friend of mine took up photography as a hobby. He took classes and acquired first-rate equipment. With this new skill, he became a free-lance sports photographer for a major university. He earns a little income, gets his expenses covered

and receives other benefits—like the best spot to watch a sports event from, such as on the floor of a basketball court.

56. Start a small business—As a retiree, your primary emphasis shouldn't be going back to work. However, some people have always wanted to run their own businesses. Your retirement years provide the perfect opportunity to do just that. But don't let it take up too much of your time and become a chore. Of course, if starting a business is too much responsibility for you, there are plenty of part-time jobs available for retirees.

57. Musical activity—A pharmacist friend of mine loved music all his life. In fifth grade he sung solos in a chorus and in high school and college he played trombone in marching bands and orchestras. Now retired, he has the time to recapture the love of music. He is in a community band that plays concerts and performs while marching in parades.

58. Substitute teaching—A guy I worked with was a marketing and advertising executive. He retired earlier than was ideal for his financial planning so he looked for some enjoyable part-time work. He became a substitute school teacher. He enjoys working with young people and the income is a nice supplement to his retirement income.

59. National Park Service work—Another military retiree I know moved to Las Vegas. For enjoyment, fresh air, and a little side income, he works part-time at Yellowstone Park, running a food stand. There are both volunteer and paying jobs with the National Park Service.

60. Coaching—Become a coach. All communities have sports for kids and teenagers that require good, talented coaches. If you ever played sports and care about sportsmanship, you can contribute your talents to helping kids develop their sports skills.

61. Umpiring and refereeing—Become a referee or umpire. I'm told that you can make some good part-time cash by working as a referee or umpire. Of course, depending on the sport, you must have good vision, you may need to be able to run, and you must know the rules of the sport. However, it can be fun and satisfying.

62. Become an adjunct professor—Most community colleges and even large universities like to have people with professional experience come in to give lectures on their specialties. Visit schools near you and pick up their schedule of classes. If you find something that you have some demonstrated expertise in, go in and talk to them. A job as adjunct professor doesn't pay well, but you may only have to go in and lecture few times a semester or quarter. However, you may find that your knowledge and experience can provide young people with a way to

make their careers more successful. Best of all, you make some part-time income teaching and enjoy the respectability of teaching at the college level. I have done both types of teaching: I have taught a college-level writing class and have just done lectures and graded papers.

63. Help repair natural disaster sites—I read a cartoon called "Stone Soup," in which the retired mom of two adult women frequently leaves home to build houses in areas that have been laid waste by natural disasters. Most recently she has been building homes in Haiti. Although a senior, she is quite competent in construction skills and has a romantic relationship with one of the other volunteers. Volunteering for this kind of charitable cause is another way that a generous retiree can find satisfaction and new friends.

64. Habitat for Humanity—For those who have construction skills or wish to develop construction skills while helping needy people, this is an excellent organization. They build houses for needy people all over the world. For information on how to volunteer to work on constructing homes in your area, see their website (www.habitat.org).

65. Utilize your particular talents—Utilize a talent or skill that you enjoy using. Many of us have abilities that provided our family income during our working lives; or we have skills or talents that we developed during our careers. Often you can use these abilities to provide a service to others or even earn a little money doing something we love to do. For instance, I helped a local high school alumni association write a history book that was extremely successful.

66. Help disadvantaged youths—As a retiree with successful life experiences, you may find it satisfying and useful to help young people, either in your own community or in problem

communities. Your wisdom and generosity can help turn people's lives around, or give young people information that can give better direction to their lives. If you have specific job knowledge, like being a welder, you can give kids an idea about how to develop valuable job skills. If you come from management, maybe you can give advice about how to get the right education or how to move up in an organization.

67. Utilize PBS pledge drives—One fun activity that you can get involved in is to participate in a PBS (Public Broadcasting System or "public TV") pledge drive. Most communities have at least one local PBS station that has periodic pledge drives. They often invite local organizations to come in and answer the phones one night during a pledge drive. However, if you don't belong to an organization that has been invited to help, they will often welcome an individual who volunteers to work. It can be lots of fun. You may get a tour of the TV station, you are often fed a meal, and you are appreciated. The staff will train you on what to do and say over the phone. The benefits you receive are that you are helping a worthy cause and your friends and family get to see you on TV.

68. Radio or TV announcing—These two ideas may seem far-fetched, but you would be surprised at the opportunities there are if you look for them. As I mentioned earlier in the book, I had the opportunity to do my own show for a non-profit local radio station. While anyone can do this, I probably wouldn't have tried if I had not done some radio work in college. However, if you have a good speaking voice, are creative, and willing to do some preparation work, it can be really exciting and fun.

69. Reawakening forgotten skills—Nearly everyone has a skill or interest that they have long forgotten, such as the radio announcing work I mentioned above. Often, in high school or

college you were involved in something you enjoyed but didn't consider for your life's work. For instance, perhaps you acted in school plays, were on the photography club, wrote for your school paper, played sports, were a singer or musician, or enjoyed some shop course you took. Why not consider picking up these skills again. I mentioned how you could get into radio, but also there are churches and community organizations that put on plays, musicals, concerts, and any number of events that would allow you to get involved. Photography can be a great hobby or part-time job. Sports can give you the opportunity to teach young people. I once served as an assistant coach for a young girls' basketball team; my school experience on a team helped me to be of some value to the girls.

70. Work in a food kitchen—Among the most satisfying of volunteer charitable experiences is to work in a food kitchen. Meeting face-to-face with the people who you are helping can be among the most fulfilling things you can do. I have never done it, but my daughter's high school class was invited to help at a food kitchen and it changed her in a most significant way.

71. Volunteer at a hospital or assisted-living facility—Volunteers at hospitals or other medical facilities for the sick or aged can be some of the most satisfying and helpful activities you can do. This kind of work is ideal for retirees because you are working with seniors and are more likely to understand their situations ("there but for the grace of God go I").

72. Other charitable causes—There are an infinite number of charitable causes you can get involved in, and there are many ways you can get involved. If you try one, and find it to your liking, it can lead to many other satisfying ways to help humanity.

73. The "Road Not Taken"—If you are open to new experiences, you may discover something you never would have thought of that is great fun or provides great satisfaction and fulfillment. One of the most unusual vacations I ever took was a Windjammer Barefoot Cruise. My wife and I sailed on a four-masted schooner with a relatively small group of adults and found an adventure that was most enjoyable and unexpected. Among other things, it was the most adult vacation we had ever been on. A company with a similar type of cruise is Island Windjammers (www.islandwindjammers. com).

74. Unusual museums—Some communities have very unusual museums that can provide specialized knowledge and experience. For instance, a local broadcast museum provides the opportunity to hear and see programs from the past, perhaps when you were a child, and even get to read the news from a teleprompter as an "anchor person."

75. Public speaking—I have some experience speaking in front of groups of people in my working life, and have been able to turn that into a retirement activity. I have moderated some events, given lectures, conducted "roasts," and just announced events. Even if you have no experience at this, you can develop a skill and develop a demand for yourself for this kind of thing.

76. Become a humorist—I have always enjoyed humor, and had some success in using humor is business and professional speaking engagements. As a retiree, I have found some new niches for humorous presentations. I do Bingo for an alumni association and make it more fun for the players by wise-cracking. I am moderator for some organizations and events and have lots of fun with that. My most recent experience was helping to "roast" a local celebrity. These are all things available to the person who develops a skill for using humor.

77. Become a handyman—If you are good with your hands, know tools, and have skills around the house, you can make a little money doing jobs for your neighbors. Or, if you prefer, you can help out elderly people who can't do their own work or can't afford to hire someone. A friend told me that the most satisfying thing he does is fix things for some of his elderly neighbors.

78. Become a docent—Docents are people who lead tours of museums, art galleries, and the like. Architectural, historic, and zoological organizations are always looking for volunteers to guide people through their exhibits. If you have special knowledge about these sorts of things, or are interested in learning about them, visit your local zoo, historical association, architectural foundation, arboretum, etc., and ask if they are looking for people to become docents. You usually have to attend

some sort of training program, but you will learn things of interest and help others appreciate the facility while on tours.

79. Become a computer repair person—If you have a skill or aptitude for computers and/or computer software, you may wish to become a computer hardware or software repair person. A friend took classes in hardware repair and now does this on the side. However, as often as not, he repairs computers for free for this senior friends who have trouble setting the clocks on their VCRs.

80. Acting in local theater—Have you ever wanted to become an actor? Well, here's your chance. Many communities, churches, and schools have annual plays or musicals. There is a need for actors and behind-the-scenes workers who have time for weeks of rehearsals. Give it a try; you could become a star; you never know.

81. Be a volunteer historian—Practically every organization needs their history researched and documented. My former employer prepared a comprehensive history for their 100th year of business, and it was done by a retiree. Schools, communities, organizations or all kinds, and churches are all looking for people to prepare histories or become authorities of their histories. Retired people, not only *look* like they know history, but they also have an appreciation for history.

82. Hunting & fishing—I don't do either of these activities, but I get the impression that fishing is not particularly demanding physically or mentally. However, a 75-year-old friend of mine goes hunting in Montana during winter and walks miles through deep snow at high altitude. He's one of the toughest guys I know.

83. Join a local service organization—I met a guy who became active in Rotary Clubs. He started out with a nominal

involvement, but it led to full-time work and high-level involvement that was very satisfying. You can be involved either in vocational activities or helping youth (see www. rotary.com). There are many such service and community clubs like this.

84. Church activities—Churches always need volunteer help that can be very satisfying to the volunteer. You may be involved in lay leadership, or fund-raising, or perhaps just a worker. All are important and provide a sense of paying back the community. A friend volunteers on the building committee for a local church; it keeps him busy and he provides a valuable service.

85. Share your expertise—There are many ways you can share the expertise you developed through your working life. This sharing often helps you to recognize how much value your experience can provide for others and it is a way to "pay back" the community for your good fortune or successful career. One organization I plan to get involved with as soon as I get a little spare time is SCORE (Counselors to America's Small Business; www.score.org). It provides the opportunity to give advice to small-business owners to help them grow.

86. Part-time work—Many retirees who need a little supplemental income or find earning a salary very satisfying may find lots of jobs available to retirees or seniors. Retail store greeters, stockers, etc., are jobs with little responsibility or stress and can be quite satisfying. However, remember that you shouldn't work just for the sake of work. Select part-time work that contributes to your happiness and self-fulfillment, but not to stress or physical exhaustion. I have had a couple of jobs that required little responsibility beyond being on time for work, and they

were enjoyable. However, don't think of them as jobs you can't quit if you become dissatisfied. It's not worth it.

87. Politics—In many communities there are opportunities for talented retirees to be elected to office. Because of your experience, you can bring great value to a political office. Also, the community is likely to have a perception that, since you are retired, you don't have a lot of financial needs and are more likely to be an honest politician. There is great opportunity for self-satisfaction in serving the community in this way, but be cautious of the downside. Communities with a lot of political corruption and dirty politics will not provide an experience you will enjoy. It's no fun to deal with crooked politicians, especially in a community that does not care about improving things for the voters.

88. Travel—One of the biggest advantages of retirement is that you have time to do things that you couldn't do while you

were working. Many retirees spend time traveling around the country visiting friends. This activity can be fun and inexpensive if you travel with friends.

89.   See the country—My father always told me that, to really appreciate our country or state, we should travel around it and see the extreme variety of scenic beauty and majesty. Retirement is an ideal time to do this, and your life-experience may give you the perspective to appreciate what you see.

90.   Horseback riding—There are many kinds of vacations that afford the opportunity to go horseback riding. I have been on rides in the Smokey Mountains and the Rocky Mountains, but

there are various kinds of rides all over the U.S., including Alaska and Hawaii.

91. Fitness adventures—There are many areas around the U.S. that have a predominance of activities that will test the fitness levels of seniors. Among the ones I have been to are east Tennessee, western North Carolina, Georgia, Maine (especially Acadia National Park), Arizona (especially the Sedona and Grand Canyon areas), Utah (especially the southeastern area near Moab), and northern California. Some of these include hiking, technical hiking, bike riding, horseback riding, rafting, canoeing and mountain-climbing.

92. Cruises—Traditional cruise ships tend toward low-impact activities onboard, but sometimes have exciting adventures during shore excursions that will give you a thrill and a workout. Among the activities I have experienced on cruises are the following: kayaking, canoeing, rafting, snorkeling, swimming, volleyball, volcano-climbing and jungle hiking.

93. Neighborhood service—Retirement often gives us the opportunity to become a good neighbor. Commuting to Chicago for 33 years kept me from having the time to get to know most of my neighbors. However, when I retired I had the opportunity to meet people in my neighborhood. Eventually, my wife and I revived an old tradition of conducting an annual neighborhood yard sale. It was not only successful, but it served to cement the neighborhood community together. Some neighbors said it was the first time they really felt a part of a neighborhood community. Of course, there are many other ways to help your neighborhood.

94. Gardening—If you have a little land around your house, you might want to spend a little time gardening, whether it is to grow flowers or vegetables. Working with nature and plants can be very satisfying and yield useful results. The fresh air and exercise will be good for you. My father-in-law really enjoyed his small garden in his senior years.

95. Home improvement—If you have skill with tools you can often find a lot of important home improvement projects around your home. These are satisfying in that you see the results of your work and save the money you'd have to spend to have them professionally done. However, if you run out of jobs to do, you'll want to plan activities to replace the work around the house. My wife has never run out of projects for me to do.

96. Creative activities—Painting and sculpting are creative activities than can awaken artistic abilities you never knew

you had. In any event, the process of creating art requires a high level of concentration that will give you much satisfaction and enjoyment. It's even possible that you may find your creations can be sold and create additional retirement income.

97. Crafts—There are any number of crafts you can be involved in if you want to balance creative activity with crafting skills. A visit to your local hobby and crafts store will provide many ideas. Among the crafts you might try are: pottery and ceramics, wood-carving, knitting, crocheting, needlepoint, quilting, macramé and tole painting.

98. Build models—It is fun and satisfying to build models of ships, planes, cars, etc. I have built scale-model plastic ships that included assembling and painting them. Other models may be made of wood or other materials. Model kits can usually be found in craft stores.

99. Learn a musical instrument—Whether or not you have ever played a musical instrument before, as a retired person you now have more time to spend with music. If you played before, you may want to learn a new instrument. If you never played before, but always wanted to, now's the time to start. This may even lead you to join a community band or orchestra.

100. Get a pet—Often people shy away from pets because of their lifestyle or because they travel. As a retired person, you now have an opportunity to adopt a pet. Especially if you are now spending more time at home, or are living alone, or have a hard time getting out, a pet can make your life more meaningful. Pets, especially dogs, provide companionship and love.

However, if you have never had a pet before, know that pets require attention and care from you. They cannot be left alone for long. However, if you will be traveling, you can always put up your pet in a kennel; many kennels provide a resort-style environment for pets.

101. Share your expertise or experience—If you belong to a professional organization, a trade union or some other organization having to do with your business, trade or profession, you may have experience or expertise that can be helpful to younger workers. Contact the appropriate organization and find out if they would be interested in having you speak, or meet with members of your business, trade or profession. It can be fulfilling and enjoyable for you, but it can be career changing for the younger people who you interact with.

102. Water skiing–I've never water-skied, but if a retiree can snow-ski, then he or she can certainly water ski. I'm thinking that water skiing has got to be fun and good exercise at the same time.

103. Cross-country skiing–This is a sport that I tried recently. It was not as much fun for me as snow skiing, but it is great exercise. Even at temperatures in the teens, I was sweating. If you live in an area that gets lots of snow, you are likely to find community and county parks, state parks and National Parks where there are trails and rental equipment available. In some ways, cross-country skiing is like hiking, but burns more calories, so it is great for weight control.

104. Ice skating—This is a sport that I did when I was much younger. A local water park has created a rink with apparatus to keep the ice frozen on warm days, so I have gotten back into it. It's fun, as well as good exercise. Best of all, it is an outdoor activity for winter.

105. Sky diving—I have never done this and I never will, but for those who relish danger and thrills, I can't imagine anything more exciting. For first timers, I understand you can jump with an instructor who makes sure your parachute opens at the right time.

106. Bungee-cord jumping—Not for the faint of heart (or me), but I understand it provides great thrills for retirees. I know several retirees who have done it and love the thrill.

107. "Zip-Trekking"–This is gaining in popularity under a variety of names. It involves hooking a person to a metal wire and gliding hundreds or thousands of feet at low or high speeds. Originally, I heard of doing this in the jungles of South America, but there are many places in the U.S. or Canada where you can do it. I have done it and found that it is fun, thrilling and safe. There is little effort involved, other than sometimes having to climb some stairs to get to the "jump off point."

108. White-water rafting–I have been white-water rafting in North
     Carolina, West Virginia and Utah, but anywhere there is a
     river with rapids and "white water," there is rafting fun. Gen-
     erally, only young people and experts will want to go white-
     water rafting on their own. The smarter, safer way is to go with
     a white-water touring company; they will give you thorough
     instructions on how to do it, how to avoid hazards, and they
     will provide a guide to get you safely through the rapids. Also,
     there are many degrees of difficulty on types of rapids, and
     the beginner my want to choose a Level Two or Three the first
     time and choose a higher level if you want greater thrills. The
     times I have gone, we have been in eight- or ten-person rub-
     ber rafts with a guide. The rapids provide thrills, and you will
     meet nice people of all ages.

109. Snow-shoeing–This is another sport I haven't yet tried, but I plan to try soon. I think it ought to be a little like cross-country skiing in that it is probably a little more rigorous than hiking. There are new kinds of snow-shoes that work better than the ones we've seen or read about in the past.

110. Water sports away from home—If you live in a warm climate on a coast, such as in Florida or California, you may wish to try some fun water activities, such as parasailing or driving a wave-runner or Jet Ski. These are easier and safer than you might think, and require little in the area of special levels of fitness. I have parasailed twice on vacations; the second time was a tandem setup in which my wife and I parasailed together. She was a little more comfortable going 500 feet up into the air when I was with her. Also, I have driven a wave-runner, and I think it is great fun for young or old.

111. Canoe trips—Two different organizations I belong to take overnight canoe trips. Typically this involves camping overnight, although there are usually motels convenient to areas for canoeing. One organization camps at a campground, rents canoes and "sit-on-tops" (which are molded plastic boats for just one person) and has meals catered by a local caterer. Members canoe for just one day and relax after that. Other organizations may have longer, multi-day, more extreme canoe trips.

112. Motorcycles—This is not my "cup of tea," but I know several retirees who travel all over the USA on motorcycles. See the Hollywood movie, "Wild Hogs," for a little idea of what it is like.

113. Marching bands—I have mentioned playing in community bands or orchestras and marching in community marching bands. I am a graduate of Purdue University and was in the Purdue Marching Band when I was a student. Purdue is a school that has band reunions every two years, and I have attended some of them. In one of them we had over 400 alumni from the ages of 20s to 70s; we marched in a football halftime show in formations with the student band. It was relatively hard work, but lots of fun remembering what it was like as a student band member. Also, I had a lot of interaction with the students. I have also marched with the Purdue All-American Alumni Marching Band during the Indianapolis 500. I understand that other universities have alumni band opportunities, and some high schools, as well.

114. Grandchildren—Whether you have grandchildren or access to other peoples' children, activities with kids can be fun. They can also be demanding and exhausting. We have taken occasional

vacations with our grandchildren, and I have had the opportunity to teach sports to my grandchildren and other young kids in the neighborhood. This can be very satisfying, because you may see the results in the kids' athletic development and success. When traveling, plan carefully with the children's parents to make sure you are prepared to make sure all of you have a good time. One of my friends spends one day a week with her grandchild, going to a variety of places, as a way of bonding.

115. Santa Claus—As I mentioned before, working or volunteering as Santa Claus or doing something similar to this can be fun and profitable. However, the greatest advantage of this is the opportunity to learn how to better interact with small children. When your own grandchildren are involved, you can create a lifetime of memories.

116. Ping-Pong—I have played this game many times—in the homes of friends and on vacation, especially on shipboard. It

is a fun, competitive sport. However, I learned from someone who vacationed in China that this sport is very popular there. I was told that Ping-Pong is great exercise, good for coordination, and superb mental exercise. I have not, as yet, verified the mental exercise part, but it is not surprising that, because of the speed of the game, players have to make a lot of rapid decisions—and thus exercise their brains.

THIS SPACE IS LEFT BLANK FOR YOU TO WRITE IN SEVERAL OF YOUR OWN IDEAS.

Note: If you discover a unique or unusual activity appropriate for retirees and want to submit it for future editions of this book, send your idea to:

Retirement Adventures

Write On Technical Writing, Inc.

417 Killarney Lane

Valparaiso, IN 46385

Include your reactions to the activity, why you liked it, an appropriate website or address for more information about it, whether it is low-impact or more active, and your contact information (in case I have questions about it I want to ask you).

Chapter Fourteen

Your Lists

As a retiree, you should have an idea about how you want to spend your time, a list of things you would like to do, and some sort of goals for achievement. Below is information for creating lists of activities you want to try and goals to set.

Your Goals

Everyone should have goals—even retirees. For instance, when I retired, I set a goal to win a gold medal at amateur downhill ski racing. I had never won anything higher than a silver medal, and I thought if I worked hard, I could improve—even as a retiree. I got in the best possible physical shape and worked on racing techniques. Not only did I win a gold medal, but I eventually qualified for the National Championships.

To create a goal, think of something you would like to excel at. Record it below and track your progress toward achieving it. Remember, achieving your goals is not the most important thing. It is the journey that counts, not the destination.

Goal No. 1

_____

Progress toward Achieving Your Goal

_____

_____

_____

Goal No. 2

_____

Progress toward Achieving Your Goal

_____

_____

_____

Goal No. 3

_____

Progress toward Achieving Your Goal

_____

_____

_____

Goal No. 4

_____

Progress toward Achieving Your Goal

_____

_____

_____

Things You Would Like to Do or Try

Most people have activities, skills or sports that they would like to try. Often, earning a living, raising a family, taking care of your home and other distractions prevent you from doing new things during your working life. Spend some time thinking about things you always wanted to do. Then make a list of several of these things. I would suggest a list of five to ten activities.

Then, make an effort to do each one. After trying something new, record your reactions. Was it something you would do again? Was it enjoyable? Did you get some value from it? Was it a disappointment?

Your reaction will tell you something about yourself. Some things you will enjoy but won't want to do again. Some things you will wish you hadn't tried. However, some things will be wonderful, and will lead you in completely new directions. Positive things will then lead you add new activities or interests to your list. I am probably a little extreme in my attitude, but I tried to do something new every week or month. Over a ten-year period, I did well over 100 new things—activities, sports, recreational activities, educational activities, travel, etc.

Make a list below of at least five things you want to try. After you try them, record your reaction.

Activity No. 1

Reactions
☐ Enjoyed Activity ☐ Would Do It Again ☐ Didn't Care For It
Comments:

Activity No. 2

Reactions
☐ Enjoyed Activity ☐ Would Do It Again ☐ Didn't Care For It
Comments:

Activity No. 3

Reactions
☐ Enjoyed Activity ☐ Would Do It Again ☐ Didn't Care For It
Comments:

Activity No. 4

Reactions
☐ Enjoyed Activity ☐ Would Do It Again ☐ Didn't Care For It
Comments:

Activity No. 5

Reactions
☐ Enjoyed Activity ☐ Would Do It Again ☐ Didn't Care For It
Comments:

Activity No. 6

Reactions

☐ Enjoyed Activity   ☐ Would Do It Again   ☐ Didn't Care For It
Comments:

Activity No. 7

Reactions

☐ Enjoyed Activity   ☐ Would Do It Again   ☐ Didn't Care For It
Comments:

Activity No. 8

Reactions

☐ Enjoyed Activity   ☐ Would Do It Again   ☐ Didn't Care For It
Comments:

Activity No. 9

Reactions

☐ Enjoyed Activity   ☐ Would Do It Again   ☐ Didn't Care For It
Comments:

Activity No. 10

Reactions

☐ Enjoyed Activity   ☐ Would Do It Again   ☐ Didn't Care For It
Comments: